The English Masonic Union of 1813

A TALE ANTIENT AND MODERN

John Belton

Published 2012 by arima publishing
www.arimapublishing.com

ISBN 978 1 84549 559 6
© John Belton 2012

Printed and bound in the United Kingdom

Typeset in Garamond

arima publishing
ASK House, Northgate Avenue
Bury St Edmunds, Suffolk IP32 6BB
t: (+44) 01284 700321
www.arimapublishing.com

cover design and art:

www.theimagedesigns.com

CONTENTS

Foreword
Freemasonry and Britishness

I am writing just a few days after the spectacular opening ceremony of the 2012 London Olympics. The eccentric and quirky ceremony produced by the Oscar winning film director Danny Boyle provided a distinctive view of British history, which embraced the Industrial Revolution and the National Health Service as well as more popular cultural references such as the Archers, Brookside and James Bond. At the very beginning of the ceremony Boyle paid tribute to the fact that Britain consists of a number of different nations by showing choirs from Northern Ireland, Wales, Scotland and England singing songs associated with each of those countries (accompanied by shots of rugby tries by each of the home nations). Yet, although Boyle (an Irish catholic who studied at Bangor University in Wales) was careful in this way to point to wider ideas of Britishness, the opening words of the ceremony were from Shakespeare, who since the early nineteenth century has been promoted as an English bard, perhaps, it has been suggested, as a counterweight to the rise of Robert Burns as the national bard of Scotland. The first scene of the Olympic ceremony showed a bucolic landscape that looked as if it was lifted from Jane Austen and was also strongly English. This pastoral scene became transformed by the building of factories with smoking chimneys. Again, this was very much an English industrial revolution, directed by Isambard Kingdom Brunel rather than the Scot James Watt or the Crawshays of Merthyr.

Yet although the opening scenes of the ceremony reflected an English – perhaps northern English – view of Britain, subsequent scenes sought to articulate a more integrated narrative of Britishness. The National Health Service, created by one of the most charismatic Welsh politicians on a model drawn from Tredegar, and which the Scottish Nationalist leader Alex Salmond has recently portrayed as a bastion of distinctively

Scottish values of fairness and collective provision, took centre stage in Boyle's Olympic Ceremony as one of the greatest British social achievements. Likewise, the emphasis of the ceremony on the multi-cultural nature of modern Britain can be seen as reflecting the growth of an idea of Britain that consists not of that 'Island Race' about which Sir Winston Churchill wrote, but rather of many different linguistic, cultural and ethnic communities engaged in a complex process of rivalry, interchange and negotiation.

I was brought up in the late 1960s and early 1970s and was taught in English schools and university where a view of 'British' history prevailed which was essentially English history, in which the Welsh, Scottish and Irish only figured when they forced themselves onto the stage, usually in a warlike or truculent fashion. Such a narrowly national view of history created huge distortions. If the 'English Civil War' is seen simply as a struggle between a monarch claiming to rule by divine right and a parliament articulating new legal interpretations of state power, then the fundamental importance in this conflict of the religious struggles in Scotland and Ireland is completely ignored. Rather than the 'English Civil War', this was a war between three kingdoms, and in order to develop a rounded understanding of this event, we need to look at the dynamic between England, Scotland and Ireland. Likewise, it is impossible to grasp the dynamics of the British Empire without seeing it as the result of a complex and frequently tetchy joint effort between English, Scots, Welsh, Irish, Cornish and many other groups.

It is no coincidence that this new awareness of British history as a history of four nations took root as the British Empire was dismantled and Britain faced huge economic and political challenges. In the 1970s, as a bitter civil conflict raged in Ulster and as Scotland and Wales agitated for devolution, books and articles began to argue for new perspectives on British history. In a fundamental lecture given in 1973, the New Zealand historian John Pocock argued for the abandonment of separate national histories for England, Scotland, Wales and Ireland and their replacement by narratives that examined the interplay between the different parts of the British Isles.[1] He proposed that it would be helpful to talk of the

---

1 J. G. A. Pocock, 'British History: A Plea for a New Subject', *Journal of Modern History* 47:4 (1975), pp. 601-621.

'Atlantic archipelago' rather than the British Isles. Likewise, in an influential book published in 1975, *Internal Colonialism*, Michael Hechter argued that England was a colonial power which had conquered other parts of the British Isles. However, in 1976 John Le Patourel in *The Norman Empire* illustrated how the complex relationships between the various parts of the British Isles cannot be reduced to simple narratives by reminding us that the Channel Islands were a legacy of a colonial power which had conquered England, namely Normandy, and discussing how this offers new perspectives on our understanding of how the Norman Conquest affected Britain more widely.

These academic arguments about British identity fed strongly into more popular studies which influenced the debate about the future of Britain, such as Tom Nairn's 1977 book, *The Crisis of Britain: Break-Up and Neo-Nationalism*. The pioneering work of scholars like Pocock and Hechter encouraged the appearance of new histories of the British Isles which sought to create a new 'four nations' narrative such as Hugh Kearney's *The British Isles: A History of Four Nations* (1989) and Norman Davies's *The Isles* (1999). The multiple levels of national myth became more evident through studies like *The Invention of Tradition* (1989), edited by Eric Hobsbawm and Terence Ranger, which showed how many of the most celebrated national emblems such as Scottish kilt and tartans or the Welsh Druidic *gorsedd* were relatively late inventions. The idea of nationality as a social construct became very influential through such celebrated studies as Benedict Anderson's *Imagined Communities* (1983) and the way in which this interplay of new and constructed perspectives on levels of national identity could produce rich new perspectives is evident in Raphael Samuel's spell-binding posthumous publication, *Island Stories: Unravelling Britain* (1998). The playful way in which Samuel explores the interplay of invention and ideas of nationality illustrates how nations use their past to give meaning to their present and future. The way in which such new perspectives on the nature of British identity can give us fresh perspectives on many different aspects of British social history is evident from Samuel's throwaway suggestions that one good way of examining the origins of Freemasonry might be to explore its similarities to the

Welsh *eisteddfodau* or that Freemasonry, by giving greater social cohesion to Scottish urban life, helped encourage Scottish separatism.[2]

I tried, in my inaugural lecture for the Centre for Research into Freemasonry at the University of Sheffield in 2001, *Freemasonry and the Problem of Britain*,[3] to suggest that the issues surrounding the historical construction and subsequent unravelling of British identity provide an important context for analyzing and exploring the history of Freemasonry. I have also attempted to explore elsewhere the ways in which Freemasonry provides a useful test bed for investigating the ways in which national identity was constructed.[4] If the history of Freemasonry is going to have any significance or interest for the wider study of history, it is of vital importance that it is placed in the context of wider historical problems such as these. However, the rise of new forms of British history is not only important in providing analytical contexts for the study of Freemasonry. 'Four kingdoms' history reminds us that it is essential for British history to study the interactions between the various ethnic, cultural and linguistic communities inhabiting these islands on the edge of the Atlantic Ocean. To study the history of the Welsh, Cornish, Scots, English, Manx or Norse separately and in isolation will always result in a partial and distorted view of history, whatever historical subject we are discussing. An old-fashioned nineteenth-century national straitjacket is an inadequate framework for developing a rounded and convincing interpretation of British Freemasonry.

The history of Freemasonry is generally written as a history of its component administrative units: of its lodges, provinces, grand lodges, chapters, supreme grand chapters and so on. This means that we are always presented with a fragmented view of Freemasonry. For example, I have argued that we cannot understand the emergence of the Mark Grand Lodge in 1856 without considering the disputes within the United Grand Lodge which were precipitated by the general political crisis

---

2 R.Samuel, *Island Stories: Unravelling Britain* (London: Verso, 1998), p. 32.

3   Available   at: http://www.scribd.com/doc/101642269/Freemasons-Problem-Sheffield-1

4 For example in 'Inventing Symbols: the Case of the Stonemasons' in *Signs and Symbols: Proceedings of the 2006 Harlaxton Conference in Memory of Janet Backhouse* ed. A. Payne and J. Cherry (Donington: Shaun Tyas, 2009), pp100-118.

caused by the poor conduct of the Crimean War.[5] Likewise, the increasing tension between the English Grand Lodge and the French Grand Orient in the 1870s was exacerbated by the activities in England of the *Loge des Philadelphes*, a group of French masonic exiles who met in London despite a prohibition of the Grand Lodge.[6] In short, we cannot analyse Freemasonry as a historical phenomenon by dividing it up into its administrative parts. We have to consider all aspects of the masonic phenomenon as a whole. In thinking about the Royal Arch at the end of the eighteenth century, it is just as important to investigate why the Ancient Order of Druids, formed in 1781, used the imagery and nomenclature of the Royal Arch as it is to investigate the records and history of the chapters of the Royal Arch associated with masonic orders.

This need for a holistic approach to the study of Freemasonry in Britain applies equally to the need to study the history of the Grand Lodges (and other masonic organisations) as a whole rather than as isolated units. Just as it is essential to study the history of this Atlantic archipelago as 'four nations' history, so likewise the history of Freemasonry must be considered as (at least) 'three Grand Lodges' history. It is for this reason that I particularly welcome John Belton's stimulating, accessible and thought-provoking reappraisal of the relationship between the Premier Grand Lodge and the Ancients Grand Lodge in England and the circumstances which prompted their Union in 1813. Ever since Henry Sadler first revealed how the origins of the Ancients Grand Lodge lay in groups of Irish and Scottish freemasons who had moved to London and been excluded by lodges belonging to the Premier Grand Lodge, it has been evident that the story of the development of the Ancients Grand Lodge and its relations with the Premier Grand Lodge up to the Union in 1813 cannot be considered in isolation from the masonic history of the rest of Great Britain. John Belton is an indefatigable researcher into Freemasonry who delights in seeking out and exploring new and provocative perspectives on the study of Freemasonry. While John's roots as a Freemason lie in the north-west

---

5 'Marking Well: Approaches to the History of Mark Masonry' in *Marking Well*, ed. A. Prescott (Hinkley: Lewis Masonic, 2006), pp5-44.

6 '"The Cause of Humanity": Charles Bradlaugh and Freemasonry', *AQC* 116 (2003), pp15-64.

of England, he has always enjoyed tasting the delights of Freemasonry in Ireland and Scotland, and John's affection for the masonic traditions of these countries is evident throughout this book. John draws together into a diverting narrative the Celtic contexts of the creation of the Ancients Grand Lodge. He then goes on to show the importance of the Scottish and Irish dimensions in interpreting the history of Freemasonry in the second half of the eighteenth century and concludes by revealing how the context of the Union of 1813 cannot be divorced from masonic events in Ireland.

This is one of the first ever attempts to give a 'four nations' perspective on the history of Freemasonry, and John cannot be congratulated highly enough on making this attempt. We will never understand the history of Freemasonry in these islands unless we break out of the old national straitjackets, and John shows how simply glancing across the Irish Sea provides us with startling new perspectives. At one level, this simply illustrates how adopting a 'four nations' perspective gives us completely new insights into British history, as can be seen by looking at the work of some of the historians I have already mentioned such as J. G. A. Pocock and Raphael Samuel. However, the story described by John also reflects the way in which historians of Freemasonry have struggled to escape from the shadow of their illustrious predecessors such as Henry Sadler or William Hughan. It seemed perhaps that Sadler, in his *Masonic Facts and Fictions* (1887), by destroying the myth perpetrated by William Preston that the origins of the Ancients Grand Lodge lay in a schism from the Premier Grand Lodge had done his work too well and said everything there was to say. Yet, much of Sadler's work reflected his attempts to draw together and organize the various records and documents that he found scattered around Freemasons' Hall in London. He paid little attention to the records of other Grand Lodges and neglected non-masonic sources, such as newspapers. John Belton shows how, if we start to explore the records of other masonic jurisdictions and examine the splendid collections of eighteenth-century newspapers which are newly available on-line, we can move considerably beyond the picture presented by Sadler.

Remarkable pioneer of masonic historiography though he was, Henry Sadler was very much a man of his time. This is illustrated by his account of the reasons for the formation of the Ancients Grand Lodge, which he ascribed to Irish pride and passion in the face of snubs from the Premier Grand Lodge:

> Does anyone at all familiar with the characteristics of an Irishman imagine that "Pat" would meekly submit to such treatment? If he does, I most decidedly do not. It seems to me much more likely that he would call some of his countrymen about him and open a lodge on his own account … One lodge would, of course, beget others, and so it probably went on until unconstituted Masonic lodges became the rallying points or centres of union of nearly all the Irish mechanics and labourers that came over to seek employment in the English metropolis.[7]

Sadler's description of the way in which these Irish lodges were formed is quite vague. John Belton's description of this process encourages us to revisit these events, and I very much hope that one of the results of John's initiative in looking again at this story will be that new contexts for understanding the emergence of the Ancients Grand Lodge will emerge. It certainly seems that the process of the creation of the Ancients Grand Lodge was by no means without antagonism. In June 1750, the clergyman and hack writer John Entick preached a sermon in the church of St Mildred in the Poultry in London which was afterwards published as *A Caution to Free and Accepted Masons*.[8] Entick warned the masonic body against the dangers of backbiting, division and dispute, and urges them to remain a united body. Given the formation of the Ancients Grand Lodge a year later, it is difficult not to read Entick's sermon as a warning against the behavior which gave rise to the formation of the Ancients Grand Lodge. Moreover, these tensions may well have had a political dimension. Entick himself was closely associated with the bookseller Jonathan Scott and the lawyer Arthur Beardmore, and from 1755 they were all associated in the writing and publication of the most notorious anti-government newspaper at the time of the Seven Years War, *The Monitor*. Indeed, Entick's rooms were searched and papers seized by government agents because of his contributions to *The Monitor*, and Entick's successful legal action against the government was seen as a landmark ruling in   the

---

7 Henry Sadler, *Masonic Facts and Fictions* (London: Diprose and Bateman, 1887), p127.

8 For all of the following, see my entry on Entick, forthcoming in *La Monde Maçonnique*, ed. C. Revauger and C. Porset.

development of the freedom of the press. Entick, Scott and Beardmore were financed by mercantile factions in London, who were anxious to protect their interests in the West Indies. Entick, Scott and Beardmore seem to have sought to use the Premier Grand Lodge from at least 1754 as a vehicle for promoting the political interests of their masters, and these three men took charge of the process of revising the *Book of Constitutions* which eventually appeared under Entick's name in 1756. It appears that wealthy London merchants with West Indian connections were seeking during the 1750s to use the Premier Grand Lodge as a vehicle to promote their political interests. This may perhaps explain Laurence Dermott's jibe that in Modern lodges tylers would draw two sign posts with chalk, 'writing Jamaica rum upon one, and Barbadoes rum upon the other'.[9]

While the Irish and Scottish contributions to the formation of the Ancients Grand Lodge are well known, less attention has been paid to the 'four nations' elements in the story of the Ancients Grand Lodge up to 1813, and it is in providing this context that John makes a fundamental contribution. In his important study of *British Clubs and Societies, 1580-1800* (2000), the distinguished historian Peter Clark analysed the respective distribution of Moderns and Ancients Lodges. He suggested that the Ancients were far more successful than the Moderns in the emerging industrial towns of the North and Midlands, and emphasised the different social profile of their membership. However, while Clark briefly compared the distribution of lodges in England and Ireland, there was scope here for a more extended 'four nations' perspective. While Clark and others have linked the growth of Freemasonry in England in the eighteenth century to urbanization, it is striking that in Scotland and Ireland there was significant masonic activity in rural areas. Given the close links of the Ancients Grand Lodge to Ireland and Scotland, it is perhaps worth wondering why rural Freemasonry failed to develop in a similar fashion in England.

The complexities and anxieties generated by Irish Freemasonry were of fundamental importance in shaping the development of Freemasonry on the British mainland, as John Belton richly illustrates. The supreme

---

9 Sadler, op. cit., p108.

flashpoint was of course the Irish Rebellion of 1798. The adoption of masonic methods of organization by the various United revolutionary groups at this time was seen by William Pitt's government as a new and terrifying means of spreading social tumult and revolution – the late eighteenth-century equivalent of Al Qaeda. With their close links to Ireland and Scotland, the Ancients Grand Lodge felt particularly at risk of revolutionary infiltration.[10] Following a meeting of the English and Scottish Grand Lodges with Pitt, the Ancients suppressed all masonic meetings except scheduled lodge and chapter meetings and ordered that brethren should disperse as soon as lodges ceased to be tyled. Nevertheless, it was the Ancients who saved the day when, as the Unlawful Societies Bill made its way through parliament, there was a risk that the amendment allowing masonic lodges to continue meeting would be defeated on constitutional grounds, so that Freemasonry would be effectively outlawed. The Duke of Atholl, Grand Master of the Ancients and a former Grand Master Mason of Scotland, leapt to the breach with a vigorous speech in defence of Freemasonry which led to a new amendment being hastily cobbled together to allow Freemasons to continue meeting – possibly the high spot in the history of the Ancients Grand Lodge and a story which John Belton recounts with great verve.

The success of the Ancients in defending Freemasonry in this way perhaps rankled at Great Queen Street. In 1802, following the collapse of talks about Union between the two English Grand Lodges, pamphlets against the Ancients Grand Lodge were printed which included copies of a series of resolutions against the Ancients passed by the Premier Grand Lodge in 1777. Robert Leslie, the Grand Secretary of the Ancients wrote to the Master of a lodge in Peterborough:

> I was wholly ignorant that the records in Queen Street contained any such personalities and reflections against His Grace the Duke of Atholl or so much rancour against our Grand Lodge. His Graces Conduct in Parliament when he recently and nobly defended the Principles of Ancient as well as Modern Masonry Merited no such New insult as the Republication and delivery of the above Letters: and if such Rancour remained upon the

---

10 For the following, see my article 'The Unlawful Societies Act of 1799' in *The Social Impact of Freemasonry on the Modern Western World*, ed. M. D. J. Scanlan, The Canonbury Papers I (London: Canonbury Masonic Research Centre, 2002), pp116-134.

Records of the Grand Lodge in Queen St it ought then if not long before been blotted out or buried in oblivion.[11]

Leslie continued:

I bear no animosity to the very respectable Grand Lodge in Queen St but they have business enough of their own without any the least interference with our Grand Lodge. By the statement of their funds published 7 April last it appears their Fund of Charity was then exhausted and in debt to their Treasurer £50 18s 3d. Their Hall has been shut up some time with a very large accumulation of debt which all our Funds Resources and Inestimable Charities great and increasing as they are - in case of a Union - must in one moment be much alienated and for ever lost with ourselves without hardly affording them even a temporary relief. They have great resources and riches in themselves competent to redeem their funds and charities without intermeddling with our Grand Lodge or its concerns...

In Leslie's view, then, the Ancients Grand Lodge was flourishing, and there was certainly no financial or other imperative which impelled them towards union with the Premier Grand Lodge. Union was only ever likely to have occurred because of overriding political anxieties at a time of great turmoil and disturbance, and this is the story which John Belton tells.

Before handing you over finally to John, one final reflection on the way in which the story of the two English Grand Lodges forms an aspect of 'four nations' history. As I have mentioned, London (oddly) did not figure significantly in the new narrative of British history presented by Danny Boyle in the 2012 Olympics. Yet London is in a way at the heart of the 'four nations' dynamic. In the eighteenth century, Wales lacked any major city, and London provided the focus of urbanization for the Welsh population. Many Welsh people went to seek work and prosperity there and it became a major centre of Welsh language culture, leading to the formation of such Welsh fraternal organisations such as the Honourable Society of the Cymmrodorion (of which, as Susan Mitchell Sommers has recently shown, the celebrated English Freemason Thomas Dunckerley was a member) and to the first appearance on Primrose Hill of Iolo Morgannwg's druidic fantasy, the Gorsedd of the Bards of the Isle of

---

11 R. Leslie to Worshipful Master and Wardens of Antients Lodge No. 160, 16 September 1802: Library and Museum of Freemasonry, Returns (SN 1600).

Britain. By contrast with Wales, Scotland possessed important and growing urban centres such as Edinburgh and Glasgow, but the role of London as a primary centre for credit made for a complex symbiosis between the mercantile classes in Scotland and London. An important Irish immigrant population had developed in London from the seventeenth century. London, in short, was a multi-cultural melting pot for Britain in the eighteenth century in much the way that it is today a multi-cultural expression of the remnants of the British Empire. In thinking about historical London, it is just as important to adopt a 'four nations' perspective as in looking at Britain more widely. This is nowhere better illustrated than in the story, so ably told by John Belton, of the Grand Lodge created by those Irish masons excluded and snubbed by their brethren and of the process which led to the Union of the two Grand Lodges two hundred years ago.

Andrew Prescott
31 July 2012

Professor Andrew Prescott FRHistS

Andrew Prescott is Professor of Digital Humanities at King's College London. From 1979-2000, Andrew was a Curator in the Department of Manuscripts at the British Library, where he acted as British Library co-ordinator for a number of digital projects, including most notably Electronic Beowulf, edited by Kevin S Kiernan of the University of Kentucky. From 2000-2007 he was Director of the Centre for Research into Freemasonry in the Humanities Research Institute at the University of Sheffield. He has also worked at the University of Wales Lampeter and University of Glasgow. After 2007 he has maintained a close and active interest in masonic research and taken a key role in the academic side of the International Conference on the History of Freemasonry. Andrew's publications include *English Historical Documents* (1988), *The British Inheritance* (with Elizabeth Hallam, 2000) and *The Benedictional of St Ethelwold: a Masterpiece of Anglo-Saxon Art* (2002). A selection of his masonic research can be found on the Pietre Stones Review of Freemasonry.

Chapter 1 - Setting the Scene

1813 is a date known to every English freemason but perversely it is also an event about which little detail is known. The basic fact is that on St John's Day in Winter of 1813 the two Grand Lodges of England, the Antients and the Moderns, joined together to become the United Grand Lodge of England. Even after a quarter-century of having been a freemason I had, until recently, not been able to shed much light upon the Union. I consulted the works of Robert Freke Gould, Bernard E Jones, Fred Pick and Norman Knight and John Hamill to find out more but they were all remarkably uncommunicative.

In trying to unpick events some two hundred years later it became clear that this was more than just an English story and that the brethren of the British Isles, be they English, Irish or Scots had all played a role. The main objective of seeking union was of course that of the joining together of two English masonic craft Grand Lodges, who managed the first three degrees. However the position in English freemasonry of the Royal Arch degree was an issue then, as it remains even today, and in the late eighteenth century so was the role played in events by the various

Knights Templar bodies. Today one can look at the structure of freemasonry and perceive it as all being well ordered and stratified; back in the eighteenth century the only Grand bodies were the craft Grand Lodges and efforts to bring order to the 'chaos' were under way. The journey was not straightforward and took many decades to resolve itself into something we would recognise today.

The (Premier) Grand Lodge of England went under several names. Typically they would simply refer to themselves as 'the Grand Lodge' but are sometimes described as the Grand Lodge of London and Westminster. By the time Anderson wrote his first Constitutions he titled them as 'The Right Worshipful Fraternity of Accepted Free Masons', and by his next edition in 1738 as 'The Antient and Honourable Fraternity of Free and Accepted Masons'. Whatever the rights and wrongs I shall stick to calling the Grand Lodge formed in 1717 the 'Moderns' and the Grand Lodge of 1751 as the 'Antients'. The canny Laurence Dermott has much to answer for, but it does demonstrate the enduring power of the brand name to influence decisions.

Gould perhaps nails his emotional colours to the mast because in Chapter XIX the chapter entitled 'History of the Grand Lodge of England According to the Old Institutions' he offers us the reminder that it is really a 'History of the Schismatics or 'Antients''. At the end of this chapter he says 'It is abundantly clear, however, that during the pendency of the Schism no other degrees were recognised by the Grand Lodges of Ireland and Scotland, than the simple *three*, authorised by the earliest of Grand Bodies'[12]. As to why there might be a Union is something Gould tiptoes around by writing 'until 1809, when it became apparent to all candid minds that the breach would soon be repaired', but alas we get no reasons for the inevitability of a Union.

Fred Pick and Norman Knight similarly only offer the thought that 'After nearly half a century of severance a new generation of freemasons of both societies had arisen, many of whom were heartily sick of the

---

[12] RF Gould (1836-1915), *History of Freemasonry*, Volume II, Chapters XIX and XX deal with the two Grand Lodges in this period. Robert Freke Gould published his three volume history between 1882 and 1887. Later editions are in larger number of volumes per set.

internecine warfare between the two bodies'[13]. More recently Hamill in his 1994 *History of English Freemasonry* makes the interesting comment that '…problems were beginning to arise in dealing with the Grand Lodges of Ireland and Scotland and the Grand Lodges appearing in Europe and the newly created United States of America, none of which appeared willing to recognise both Grand Lodges in England'.[14] As we shall see later the Antients mostly had it their own way in the relationships with Ireland and Scotland and for reasons which may be simply explained.

William James Hughan, like Gould, an avid masonic researcher and founder member of Quatuor Coronati Lodge No.2076, does record the events of the Union in print in his *Memorials*[15] but since then these events have remained in the shadows pretty much unseen by researchers. When Hughan wrote his *Memorials* in 1874 and Gould completed Volume II of his *History* in 1886 it was still in the early days of more systematic masonic research and it was the 'authentic' school of masonic history and the 'ancient charges' that were the more popular topics than more relatively recent events.

This effort to shed some light upon the eventual union of Moderns and Antients really starts around 1751 when a dozen or so independent lodges came together to form the Antients Grand Lodge.

Hughan had a view, which was that 'The precise origin of the secession of 1730-1752 has not yet been exactly ascertained, but we may safely assume that the disagreement which arose was mainly fostered by the operatives, in whose practical minds the institution of the Society of Free and Accepted Masons on a cosmopolitan basis was evidently regarded as directly opposed to their ancient customs and privileges.'[16] Sadly he gives no clue as to his evidence for this statement.

---

[13] FL Pick and GN Knight (with later editions by Frederick Smyth), *The Pocket History of Freemasonry*, p105 in the 1992 edition. This book ran to nine editions between 1953 and 1991, which must be a mark of its excellence. Sadly still nothing has replaced this excellent work for offering a broad sweep of masonic history across the British Isles and round the world.

[14] J Hamill, *History of English Freemasonry* (1994), p59

[15] William James Hughan (1841-1911), *Memorials of the Masonic Union of 1813*, (1874) and revised edition 1913. PDF versions of these are available online.

[16] WJ Hughan, *Memorials*, p4

It is common when writing the history of freemasonry to deal with the masonic histories of England, Ireland or Scotland as being totally separate and distinct but the reality is that they are not separate and neither can they be separated from the national histories of the 'tribes' of the British Islands which came together and then parted time after time. They offer the context for the events that follow and a few notes on the histories of the nations of the British Isles seem essential background to further exploration. They were as tightly entangled then as they still are today!

There had of course been a Union of the Crowns since 1603 when the Stuart King James became the monarch of both England and Scotland, while both countries retained their parliaments. Then as now there were tensions, over trade and over finance. There was an attempted Act of Settlement emanating from England in 1701 which haggling delayed until 1707 while the Scots sought better terms. Scotland had suffered grievous financial losses in the Darien Scheme[17] of the 1690s and also felt that it was seriously behind England in terms of growth and prosperity. While a union with England found little favour with a majority of Scots, its politicians saw their economic future being closely linked with that of England and that such a link would also protect Scottish Protestantism. Thus from 1707 England and Scotland (while continuing to be known officially as Great Britain) began to be referred to informally as the United Kingdom of England and Scotland.

It was to be almost another century before Ireland became a political part of what would become the United Kingdom of Great Britain and Ireland. It was the unrest in Ireland which, in 1798, broke out into the open rebellion of the United Irishmen that resulted in the decision of the British Government to incorporate Ireland into Great Britain. This was an attempt at both union and catholic emancipation and opinion in Ireland was much divided. Some supported Union but against Catholic Emancipation while others were in favour of both. Eventually a deal was

---

[17] The plan was to establish a colony on the Isthmus of Panama to turn Scotland into a major trading nation. It was abandoned in 1700 after a decade of effort. The attempt however consumed about a quarter of Scotland's monetary resources. This combined with a series of bad harvests eventually led to the Act of Union with England of 1707. Scotland thus gained access to the markets of the 'English empire' and prospered as a result.

struck and the Irish Parliament voted for the change, and its own abolition, and the Union became effective in January 1801.

Wherever I turned in trying to work out just what influences were at work in English freemasonry I kept tripping over noble Grand Masters with either strong Scots or Irish roots. Of the Grand Masters of noble ancestry in the original Grand Lodge between 1717 and 1751 two of the seventeen were Irish and five were Scots, and in the period between 1751 and 1813 out of a total of nine Grand Masters three were Irish Peers. For the Antients, of the five noble Grand Masters two were Irish and three were Scots. Thus out of a total of thirty one Grand Masters fifty percent were not English nobility with almost a quarter being Scots, and a quarter Irish. This is a somewhat surprising tally and as the tale progresses a number of these will appear as characters who played important parts in key events in the development of English freemasonry.

One has to be surprised that so many Grand Masters of the English Grand Lodges were not English. Did the English nobility find masonry less pleasing than those of Ireland or Scotland or were there just fewer of them? Was freemasonry in Ireland and Scotland more socially significant and predominant than in England which meant that more nobility were available to be chosen? Those are questions to be answered elsewhere but the thought that there was significant Irish and Scots influence might prompt us to take a more 'British Isles' view of events rather than a purely parochial English view of Masonic history. This closeness, if not always unanimity of view and style, between the Grand Lodges is still mirrored today in the use of the term 'The Three Home Grand Lodges'. But the context for all of this was partly set by great events in Europe.

The final decades of the 18th century were troubled times in Europe. Louis XVI came to the throne of France in the middle of a financial crisis, near bankruptcy and with expenditure exceeding income. France had spent vast sums of money during the Seven Years War (1756-1763) and in support of the Americans in their Revolutionary War (1775-1783). It was attempts to raise more taxes that eventually sparked off trouble. The French Revolution ran from 1789-1799 with the Bastille being stormed in July 1789, a republic proclaimed in 1792, and King Louis XVI executed the next year. The whole revolution became radicalised and during the Reign of Terror between 16,000 and 40,000 people were killed and Napoleon came to power in 1799.

Britain dealt with the revolt of the United Irishmen in 1798 and had been at war with France from 1793 till 1802, and again at war with France in 1803, a war that lasted till 1815. There was the famous naval battle of Trafalgar won by Nelson in 1805, Napoleon's retreat from Moscow in 1812 and the final showdown at Waterloo in 1815. Just for good measure Britain was also at war with the United States from 1812-1815 (during which, in 1814, the British burnt the building which when repainted became the White House). The French Revolution had greatly affected the social and political scene in England. The likelihood that Britain would have a French-style revolution in Britain remains a matter of controversy to this day. However in May 1800 there was an attempted assassination of King George III in the Drury Lane Theatre by firing a gun at the King while the National Anthem was being sung. It failed and it was later discovered that the would-be assassin James Hadfield was not motivated by politics but was deemed deranged and having got in with a religious sect – he was acquitted. Grand Lodge was moved to quickly send an address to His Majesty expressing their great pleasure at his deliverance from danger.

There were however a number of intellectuals who espoused a radical cause and sought social change. It is worth naming some of them for they are names still well known today. William Wordsworth (1770-1850), poet, visited France in 1791, author of 'I wondered lonely as a cloud' commonly known as 'The Daffodils'; Samuel Taylor Coleridge, poet and author of the 'Ancient Mariner'; Percy Bysshe Shelley, poet and radical; Thomas Paine, author of *The Rights of Man* and who somehow or other managed to be either in America or France for their revolutions; and Joseph Priestley[18], scientist and Unitarian. These were all men who could

---

[18] Joseph Priestley, born into a dissenting family, taught languages and rhetoric at the Warrington Academy from 1761-1767 and studied electricity, elected a Fellow of the Royal Society in 1766. He moved around taking employment as a minister of dissenting chapels. In Calne in Wiltshire he became a founder of Unitarianism in 1774, announced the discovery of oxygen in 1776 and moved to Birmingham where he stayed from 1780-1791. He became a member of the Lunar Society which contained many of the movers and shakers of the industrial revolution, men such as Matthew Boulton (industrialist),

gain the ear of the populace and influence opinion and the government were of course much concerned. Edmund Burke (1729-1797), Irish, MP, statesman, orator, philosopher and freemason; while being opposed to revolution was also able to raise the level of debate on matters concerning British society.

Reform was to come later in the nineteenth century but the industrial revolution was radically changing the wealth and power base of the country. The need for some national response to the pressures within society was becoming ever more pressing, both from internal socio-economic developments and radical changes in Europe. All the events which led up to the Union of 1813 have to be viewed in the social background of the times. While men may be masons in tyled lodge rooms once they come out they have to feed their families and educate their children just like everyone else. The great events of the day and their fears and worries all influenced attitudes – of freemasons as much as non-freemasons.

Any mason whose interests have gone beyond the three Craft degrees will almost certainly know that the way in which the Chapter degrees are organised in England is unique in the Masonic world. It is based upon a concept of 'Pure Ancient Freemasonry' which declares that the degree of the Holy Royal Arch is not really a degree but rather the completion of the third degree. This curiosity will be explored in more detail in the book and with reference to events elsewhere which led to this stance being adopted in England. It is normal to consider that just as the Craft and its structures seem to have existed from time immemorial that the organisation of the other degrees has been likewise of long standing. This, both for the Royal Arch and Knights Templar, has been emphatically not the case; one might best describe the custom and practice at the end of the eighteenth century as being akin to a masonic 'Wild West'.

The Scottish Rite does not feature here because it was a late arrival and played no real part in the events that led up to the English Masonic Union of 1813. Neither does the Mark degree, not because something

---

James Watt (steam engines and a freemason), Josiah Wedgwood (of the eponymous pottery) and Benjamin Franklin (American patriot, scientist and freemason).

called the Mark was absent from freemasonry, just simply because it did not play a role in the controversies that led to the Union of 1813.

While this book is primarily a celebration of the Bicentenary of the formation of the United Grand Lodge of England in 1813 it is also perhaps a celebration of the interactions of the various masonic bodies across the British Isles and most especially of all those masons, who over many decades, have contributed to our history.

Frontispiece of Ahiman Rezon, 1764 Edition

Chapter 2 – The Antients Grand Lodge

Anyone who has read what has been written regarding the earliest origins of freemasonry will be well aware of the competing claims between England and Scotland. Such claims do tend to become very nationalist in nature but fortunately such debates can be put aside because this book deals with events after 1751 by which time independent freemasonry is firmly established in each of the nations of Britain. As the British Empire grew it became very much a process that involved all the peoples of the British Isles and this book starts by applying that thought and principle to Masonic activity

It is however worth touching upon three early occasions when men were made masons who were not (stone) masons by profession. On 20th May 1641 some members of the Scottish army near Newcastle upon Tyne who were members of the Lodge now called Lodge of Edinburgh (Mary's Chapel) No.1 initiated "the right honerabell Alexander Hamilton general off the artelerie off theis kingdom and Mr thie Right honerabell Mr

Robert Moray, General Quarter Mr to the armie off Scotland". Five years later Elias Ashmole records in his diary that on 16 October 1646 "I was made a Free Mason at Warrington in Lancashire, with Coll: Henry Mainwaring of Karincham in Cheshire". Finally to mention the case of Randle Holme III of Chester who left documents in which he declared himself to be a Free Mason of a lodge in Chester and who probably became a freemason around 1665. These men being made masons during or just after the Civil War in England does at least indicate that it was at last possible in society in Britain for new organisations to form and to undertake intellectual exploration without persecution. Likewise the Royal Society prospered and was surely instrumental in stimulating Britain into a more scientific time which resulted in it then developing into an industrial powerhouse.

In 1716 four London lodges meeting at the Goose and Gridiron, the Crown Ale-house, the Apple Tree Tavern and the Rummer and Grapes Tavern together with some older brothers met and agreed to form a Grand Lodge. Although the accepted date for this is 1717 they did not start to record minutes of their meetings until 1723. The first lodges that joined all met in London and Westminster but eight years later the list included Lodges in Bath, Bristol, Chester, Chichester, Gosport, Salford, Norwich and Warwick, and by 1728 lodges were being founded overseas as well. The question remains of course as to where these lodges appeared from. It would seem likely that lodges existed in many parts of the country and that some of these independent lodges decided to join the new Grand Lodge. It is also probably true that there were other lodges that remained independent and simply continued making masons as they had always done – and of course there was the Grand Lodge of All England at York which expired around 1792.[19]

---

[19] The Grand Lodge of All England at York seemingly started as an operative lodge which became speculative. Its earliest records as a lodge are dated 1712 and in 1725 it is recorded as electing a Grand Master and two Grand Wardens. While it got a mention in the Anderson Constitutions of 1738 it became dormant between 1740 and 1760, and only at the later date did it start warranting lodges. It only warranted some 14 lodges and one Grand Lodge and the geographical spread was limited to Yorkshire, Lancashire and Cheshire. It faded and lingered on until around 1792 and thus played no part in the events that led up to 1813.

There have always been differing views of what lay behind the creation in 1751 of the Antients Grand Lodge. There seems to be a general agreement that the management of the Moderns Grand Lodge was below par, and it may be that the roles of Grand Secretary and Grand Master were not sufficiently defined to meet the rapidly developing needs of the organisation. The Grand Mastership of the 3rd Lord Byron, between 1747 and 1752, is often quoted as an example of inefficiency as he spent most of his time abroad. It seems that after his Installation in April 1747 he did not again attend Grand Lodge until March 1752, the meeting at which his successor was selected.

There can be little doubt that various exposures, but particularly Samuel Prichard's 1730 *Masonry Dissected*, caused consternation about who was getting admitted to meetings of lodges. It was the sheer popularity of *Masonry Dissected* in which the words of a ritual were clearly displayed that gave rise to quite reasonable fears for the secrets and for imposters to gain use of Masonic charity. By around 1739 Grand Lodge had decided that it had to take some action and it decided to reverse the words of the first and second degrees. Whether this was a wise thing to do or not can be debated at length but it did create a situation upon which the Antients Grand Lodge would late capitalise.

The word schism is often used when describing events around the creation of the Antients Grand Lodge. However there is no evidence that any lodges belonging to the 1717 Grand Lodge actually left to create a new grand lodge. As Bernard Jones writing in the 1950s says:

> For upwards of a century the formation of the rival Grand Lodge was referred to as a schism, and the men who formed it as seceders. 'Schism' is literally a 'splitting' or 'cleavage'; a 'seceder' is one who formally withdraws from membership of a body. We have plenty of evidence now to prove that the event was not a schism, for a while there may have been and probably were, a number of Brethren who went over to the rival body, for the main part that body which came into existence as a result of the determined efforts of Irish and Scottish masons residing in England, helped by English masons who for the most part had never owed allegiance to the first Grand Lodge.[20]

---

[20] Bernard E Jones, *Freemasons Guide and Compendium* p196. First published in 1950 and reprinted on many occasions until the 1980s. This excellent book and its companion

The Minutes of the Moderns Grand Lodge of 11th December 1735 record that:

> Notice being given to the Grand Lodge that the Master and Wardens of a Lodge from Ireland attended without, desiring to be admitted, by virtue of a Deputation from the Lord Kingston present Grand Master of Ireland. But it appearing that there was no particular Recommendation from his Lordp in this affair their request could not be comply'd with, unless they would accept of a new Constitution here.[21]

Perhaps the words of the Irish Masonic researcher John Heron Lepper throw a non-English point of view on matters when he says that 'The body of malcontents gradually increased with every Irish mason who left his country for his own or his country's good, and with every Scotch Mason who found the view from the high road leading into England a finer piece of scenery than any to be discovered at home.'[22] Perhaps we should countenance the thought that immigrant Irish and Scots masons were not finding themselves welcomed into Lodges of Englishmen and that they did what all immigrant communities do – they simply formed their own societies to meet their needs.

Some questions are, sadly, unlikely ever to be answered. We cannot know of those lodges which founded the Antients whether the 'immigrant' members came to England as masons or were made here and neither can we know exactly why they felt unwelcomed in existing lodges. Thus it was that on Wednesday 17th July 1751 a General Assembly of lodges 'met (at the Turks Head Tavern in Greek Street, Soho) to revive the Ancient Craft'. They appointed a committee which formulated a code of sixteen Rules and Orders. The first Secretary did not keep minutes, or if he did they have not survived.

The next momentous step is recorded briefly in the first Minute Book, and it is worth reading:

Freemasons Book of the Royal Arch are recommended reading and are available on the second hand market.

[21] *Quatuor Coronati Antigrapha (QCA)* Vol.X p259.

[22] John Heron Lepper, *Fraternal Communications between the Grand Lodges of England and Ireland in the 18th Century*, p5 'On causes of estrangement'. Privately published and undated booklet but date stamped 1924. Ref B 105 LEP in the Library and Museum of Freemasonry, London.

Transactions of the Grand Committee
Of the Most Ancient and Honourable Fraternity
Of Free and Accepted MASONS

At the Griffin Tavern in Holborn London Feb the 5th 1752

Mr James Hagarty in the Chair

Also Present the Officers of No.2, 3, 4, 5, 6, 7, 8, 9, & 10 being Representatives of all the Ancient Masons in and adjacent to London.

Brother John Morgan Secretary informed the Committee that he being lately appointed to an Office on board one of His Majesty's Ships, he Rec'd Orders to prepare for his departure and therefore advised the Grand Committee to chuse a new Secretary immediately.

Upon which Brother John Morris past Master of No.5 and Brother Laurence Dermott of No.9 and 10 and Past Master No.26 Dublin were proposed and admitted as Candidates for the Office of Grand Secretary. And Grand Secretary Morgan was Ordered to Examine the Candidates separately and report his opinion of their Qualifications.

After a long and minute Examination Relative to Initiation, passing, Installations, and General Regulations &c. &c. &c. Brother Morgan declared that Brother Laurence Dermott was duly qualified for the Office of Grand Secretary. Whereon the Worshipful Master in the Chair put up the Names of John Morris and Laurence Dermott, separately when the latter was Unanimously Chosen Grand Secretary: and accordingly he was Installed in the Ancient Manner.[23]

What we can discover is that there were ten lodges in London, and possibly others outside but not part of the Grand Committee, and that they elected Bro Laurence Dermott as Grand Secretary. Dermott was eventually to act as Grand Secretary until 1771 and then until 1787 was often elected as Deputy Grand Master. Because he has left an indelible mark upon English freemasonry it is worth looking at his background and life. He was born in Ireland in 1720, initiated at the age of 20, and became Master of Lodge No.26 in Dublin in 1746. He was exalted into the Royal Arch on the 16th April 1746. He came to England around 1748 and worked as a journeyman painter and it is often stated that he first joined a lodge in the Moderns Grand Lodge – although there is alas no evidence for this. He clearly had some education but it was his active style and energy that made him, and thus the Antients, a real match for the efforts

---

[23] *QCA* Vol. XI, *Early Records of the Grand Lodge of England according to the Old Institutions,* p29-30.

of the Moderns in their efforts to promote their society. He started the publishing of a book of constitutions entitled *Ahiman Rezon, or A Help to a Brother,* which ran to three more editions under his editorship and a further four before the Union of 1813. It is perhaps the fact that he was exalted into a Royal Arch Chapter in Dublin that accounts for some of the enthusiasm of the Antients for the Royal Arch; but there must as well have been a thirst among brethren for other further degrees. The Royal Arch seems to just have been a degree that came to be included as part of what lodges did, and of course took a fee for as well.

The Antients Grand Committee met again in March 1752. In the minutes of the meeting it is recorded that they examined the case of two men Thomas Phealon and John Macky who allegedly seldom met twice at the same alehouse but made masons for the consideration of a leg of mutton for dinner. They were both accused of being 'imposters in Masonry' and in particular of making Royal Archmen while not having 'the least Idea of that Secret' and also of telling 'a long story about 12 white Marble stones &c. &c. and that the Rainbow was the Royal Arch, with many other absurdities equally foreign and ridiculous'. The finding was that 'neither Thomas Phealon nor John Mackey be admitted into any Ancient Lodge during their natural lives'. This certainly seems to imply that many of the Antient masons were familiar with the details of the Royal Arch.

One further mention of the Royal Arch is required because it marks a clear intent to bring better order to the Royal Arch and occurs in the Antients meeting of 2nd March 1757:

> Order'd the Masters of the Royal Arch shall also be Summon'd to meet in Order to regulate things relative to that most valuable branch of the Craft

There can however be no doubt at all of Dermott's view of the importance of the Royal Arch for in *Ahiman Rezon* he writes about:

> That part of Masonry commonly called the Royal Arch (which I firmly believe to be the root, heart and marrow of masonry.)[24]

Things were moving on for in April they had asked Lord George Sackville to become Grand Master. He declined, but only because the

---

[24] *Ahiman Rezon: A Help to a Brother.* In the second London edition it appears on p47 and seems to be in all the editions.

Grand Lodge of Ireland had chosen him as Grand Master, but said that he would accept upon his return to England. In September they agreed that the Grand Secretary might issue Dispensations and Warrants for preserving and augmenting the Ancient Craft but that they must be confirmed by the next Grand Master.[25] In October they agreed 'that the Craft flourish'd most and best when Governed by a Noble Grand Master' and in the following month they had a shortlist of the 'Rt. Honble, Lords Chesterfield, Ponsonby, Inchquin and Blesinton'. The minutes indicate that there was much discussion about such matters as having suitable premises for a feast after installing a Noble Grand Master, finances and the purchase of a set of candlesticks. As a result the matter of a Noble Grand Master got delayed for a couple of years.

It was not until the Grand Lodge meeting on December 1st 1756, almost some four years later, that the matter was addressed and finally resolved.

> The Grand Lodge proceeded to the choice of Gd. Master &c when the Rt. Honorable William Stewart Earl of Blesinton was Unanimously chosen Gd. Master &c.
>
> Orderd that the Grand Secretary shall write a letter of thanks
>
> To the Rt. Honble. Earl Blesinton for his Ldships great Condescension and humbly beg his Ldship will please appoint his Deputy &c.[26]

William Stewart, the Earl of Blesinton, was duly installed although by proxy as he could not be present in person – and he served until 1760. It might easily slip past one's attention that before 1745 the Earl of Blesinton had been the 3rd Viscount Mountjoy. It was in that earlier incarnation that he had been the Grand Master of Freemasons in Ireland from 1738-40. Perhaps therefore we should not be surprised to read the following in the minutes of 1st March 1758.

> Heard a letter from Mr John Calder (GS) in Dublin wherein he assured the Grand Lodge of Antient Masons in London that the Grand Lodge did

---

[25] This practice of issuing Dispensations for lodges was not a feature of Modern masonry but the Antient practice still functions today in, for example, North America, where lodges operate under dispensation and if they are found to be functioning well they are then Constituted. The practice no longer exists in England where a lodge may now not meet until after it is Consecrated.

[26] *QCA* Vol.X, p69. The exchanges went on at some length.

mutually concur in a strict Union with the Antients in London and promised to keep a Constant Correspondence with them.

Order'd that the Grand Secretary shall draw up an answer in the most Respectful and Brotherly Terms wherein the General thanks of this Grand Lodge shall be convey'd, and assure them that we will to the Utmost of our powers promote the welfare of the Craft in General.

And again at the Grand Lodge meeting of 1762, presumably after correspondence from Ireland had been missed.

Heard a letter from Grand Secretary Calder in Ireland in answer to the former letter written by Secretary Dermott to the Grand Lodge of Ireland proposing a Continual Correspondence

Order'd: That a Continual Correspondence[27] shall be maintained with the Grand Lodge of Ireland

Thinking about events it is entirely logical that William Stewart, having previously been Grand Master in Ireland, would wish that the other Masonic body of which he now found himself Grand Master would be on speaking terms with his previous one. He would expect to be able to go between one and the other as he chose without let or hindrance. Perhaps the only surprise is that it took so long to establish 'constant correspondence'[28]. One might suspect that in the beginning this was viewed by the Antients as a small matter. By 1762 they almost certainly saw this as a key part of their strategy in gaining ascendency over the Moderns. After all if Ireland were in Constant Correspondence with them

---

[27] Today we tend to view things like Regularity and Recognition as very black and white matters and words like irregular and clandestine are bandied about – they are sullying and unpleasing words and intended to be so. In the eighteenth century Masonic world such matters were still new and little tested. It was probably simply because noble Brethren were or had been Grand Masters in more than one place that some form of acknowledging amity had to be found. The chose to call it 'Constant Correspondence' and at the simplest level it was to send each other copies of their minutes; but as we have already seen without some sort of amity admission into lodges became problematic. It could be argued that Irish masons gained by getting access to Antients lodges while the Antients gained because the Moderns credibility was reduced.

[28] Actually this was not the first example of 'constant correspondence', i.e. recognition, occurring. In Scotland on 1st December 1740 the Right Honourable Thomas, Earl of Strathmore and Kinghorn, was elected Grand Master. Also at the meeting 'It was proposed, and unanimously agreed to, that a correspondence should be opened between the Grand Lodge of Scotland and the Grand Lodge of England, and that the assistance of the latter in building the Royal Infirmary should be particularly requested.'

then they would not and could not be in Constant, indeed any, Correspondence with the Moderns. The position of the Antients was safely maintained!

Cadwallader 9ᵗʰ Lord Blayney (1720-75) Co Monaghan, Ireland.
Grand Master (Moderns) 1764-1766

Chapter 3 - Royal Arch Charter of Compact 1766

The Charter of Compact of 22nd July 1766 which formed the *Excellent Grand and Royal Arch Chapter of Jerusalem* seems clouded in controversy wherever one looks. Even its name is often misquoted as the Supreme Grand Royal Arch Chapter of England, but it did change its name in 1798 to the Grand Lodge of Royal Arch Masons and then in 1801 to Supreme Grand Chapter.

Whenever and wherever a Grand Master of the Moderns is written about the reader is invited to assume that the Noble brother is a Peer of the (English) Realm, but this was not always the case. Cadwallader 9th Lord Blayney was born in Ireland on 2nd May 1720 and died in Cork on 13th November 1775 – a Peer of Ireland. He received a military education at military academies in France and Germany and the family had other earlier masonic connections. He rose through the ranks of the military ending up as Lieutenant General in 1772. He was Grand Master of the

Moderns[29] between 1764 and 1766 and after that was elected as Grand Master of the Grand Lodge of Ireland on 6th May 1768 but resigned before his Installation.[30] It is said that he never after that entered any lodge; but the reasons for this remain shrouded in mystery.

The mere fact that by 1766 there was sufficient pressure to create a Royal Arch organisation tells us that while the Antients might have been promoting it as 'the root, heart and marrow of freemasonry' it had also taken root within the masonry of the Moderns as well. A few words are really needed on the origins of the Royal Arch degree and these will be presented going backwards in time presenting the less certain thoughts last.

As Bernard Jones says[31] 'their (the Moderns') official attitude of indifference to the Royal Arch may have largely turned, as the years went by, upon the zealous adoption by their opponents of the 'new' ceremonial'. Clearly the Royal Arch was already being practised before the Antients formed their Grand Lodge – Dermott himself was Exalted in 1746 in Dublin. In terms of minutes and printed references there is of course *Faulkner's Dublin Journal* of January 1744 giving an account of a procession in Youghal, County Cork, Ireland when "the Royal Arch was carried by two Excellent Masons" and when Fifield D'Assigny[32] describes worthy men as being 'Masters of the Royal Arch'. In Scotland there is

---

[29] In November 2010 the Irish Lodge of Research visited Castleblaney and the paper at this meeting comments (in a delightfully Irish unreferenced way) that 'Lord Blayney set himself two goals to be completed during his tenure as Grand Master firstly, to extend the repute and power of the Premier Grand Lodge of England and secondly, to restore the 'Antient' forms of ritual wherever they had been discarded with a view to reconciliation between the 'Antient' and 'Modern' Grand Lodges'.

[30] The only record of this event, and indeed only one copy survives, is in the title page of the official supplementary Rules and Regulations, a document of 16 pages only, of the Grand Lodge of Ireland published in 1769. It records his election and under the date of 24th June 1768 'Lord Blayney having resigned, the Earl of Cavan was re-elected G.M.' In JH Lepper and P Crossle *History of the Grand Lodge of Ireland*, Volume 1 (1925).

[31] Bernard E Jones, *Freemasons' Book of the Royal Arch*. This is pretty much the only book devoted in its entirety to the Royal Arch. First published in 1957 and reprinted till 1986 it represents a great resource for those with an interest in the Royal Arch even if some of the views expressed do look today a little dated.

[32] W J Hughan in his *Masonic Memorials of 1813* (1874) also includes the text of D'Assigny's *Serious and Impartial Inquiry*. It is also worth noting that D'Assigny says that in Dublin the Royal Arch was claimed to have been brought from York (England).

note of a Royal Arch ceremony being worked in Stirling in 1743 and 1745; it is recorded that two brothers 'being found qualified, they were admitted Royal Arch Masons of this Lodge'.

In England there is of course Thomas Dunkerley's claim that he was Exalted in a Portsmouth Lodge in 1754 – and he of course was a Modern Mason! The sad and curious case of John Coustos does deserve our consideration, especially as his statements were recorded in detail. The Pope Clement's Papal Bull of 1738 attempted to close down freemasonry and as a result of this, in 1742-3, John Coustos, Master of a lodge in Lisbon, was denounced to the Inquisition. Coustos was Swiss by birth, English by adoption and had been initiated in London in 1730. He was arrested and questioned on several occasions and in April 1744 was tortured on the rack and sentenced to serve four years on the galleys. Part of his evidence does seem to relate to the Royal Arch degree:

> ...when the destruction took place of the famous Temple of Solomon there was found below the First Stone a tablet of bronze on which was engraved [the word 'JEHOVAH'] meaning 'GOD'...[33]

These pieces of evidence have their detractors but when taken together it becomes harder to disbelieve an origin earlier than that date for the Royal Arch degree. In this spirit readers might like to consider pages 9-16 of Andersons Constitutions of 1723. Here are set out by the writer, generally believed to be Dr James Anderson (with the preface by Dr Desaguliers), in the text and footnotes, is a Traditional History of Freemasonry. Thus we can read about the construction of King Solomon's Temple, of Adoniram, Hiram King of Tyre and of Hiram Abif and mention of the tribes of Israel. And later of the destruction of the Temple of Solomon by Nebuchadnezzar, and of the Jews who constructed the Hanging Gardens of Babylon afterwards returning to Jerusalem, and then of the story of the rebuilding of the Temple by Zerubbabel. The inclusion of these references perhaps pushes one to consider the possibility that by 1723 both the Hiramic legend and thus the Third Degree <u>and</u> also the Royal Arch were already in the minds of

---

[33] S Vatcher, *John Coustos and the Portuguese Inquisition* in *AQC* Vol.81 (1968) pp9-87. This account goes into considerable detail, and it also refers extensively to John Coustos' own book *The Sufferings of John Coustos* published in London in 1746 and reprinted in 1790. Again this book is currently available free online as a PDF.

the writers of the Constitutions of 1723 (if not even actually being worked).

A Scots Masters' Lodge was recorded as meeting in London in 1733 and also Scots Masters degrees were worked elsewhere that were not of the normal Craft nature. Possibly these workings originated in France, and were called Scots perhaps because of Scottish refugees there. The Scots Master degree had a feature which according to Gould included 'the discovery in a vault by Scottish Crusaders of the long lost and ineffable word – also that in this search they had to work with the sword in one hand and the trowel in the other. The epoch related to is, however, that of the Crusades not that of Zerubbabel's (or the Second) Temple'.[34] He goes on to add that 'at this distance in time it would be impossible to define their (the degrees) precise teachings'.

The desire of freemasons to find other degrees had perhaps started by the addition of the Master Mason degree in the 1720s and seemingly in the 1730s the Royal Arch. One has to remember that there was little organisation and structure in freemasonry at this time and freemasons must have felt free to find new experiences without many constraints. Formal bodies to offer Charters or Warrants were still largely in the future. The Masonic experience was within the lodge and, of course, the lodge charged a fee for conferring each and every other degree. To avoid getting the monetary side out of context it is clear from the increasing number of references to the Royal Arch degree that brethren across Britain were keen to join.

What turned out eventually to be a multiplicity of degrees, none of them being controlled by Grand Lodges, was becoming a threat to the established order. If the centre of freemasonry was the three Craft degrees then the place of other degrees would have to be determined at some time. Maybe when Grand Secretary Spencer said that the Royal Arch was 'an innovation...to seduce the brethren'[35] he was the first to

---

[34] R F Gould, *History of Freemasonry* (1887) Vol.3 p92.

[35] The Moderns less approving stance was epitomised on several occasions by their Grand Secretary, Samuel Spencer, writing, in 1759, to an Irish brother seeking charity, that 'Our Society is neither Arch, Royal Arch or Antient' and in 1767 that 'The Royal Arch is a society we do not acknowledge and which we hold to be an invention to

identify the problem, one which would only get addressed fully in the first half of the nineteenth century. The problem was the conflict between the brethren who enjoyed being 'seduced' by other and newer degrees and Grand Lodges who felt they were loosing control.

The Antients had dealt with this by including the Royal Arch within their Grand Lodge. Thus the appearance of a Grand and Royal Arch Chapter in 1766 through the Charter of Compact was one way that the Royal Arch faction within the Moderns sought to regularise this degree. As Bernard Jones says '(Grand Chapter) was probably as warmly welcomed by the rank and file as it was resented by some of their leaders and officials'.

Lord Blayney was elected in absentia as Grand Master in April 1764 and only returned and was present in Grand Lodge in January 1766 and at two further meetings that year. On 11th June he was exalted in the Excellent Grand and Royal Chapter and effectively became head of the Royal Arch. It would seem that the idea of a Charter was discussed on the 2nd July and the draft of the Charter of Compact agreed on the 22nd of July[36]. At the meeting of the 30th July Samuel Spencer, the Grand Secretary, and the Grand Treasurer were both present as visitors. Spencer was elected a member of the Chapter but never paid his joining fee, never appeared on the list of members and never attended again. At some time in the next couple of years the date on the Charter of Compact was changed with the final digit in 1766 becoming a 7 and the letters GM after Lord Blayney's name becoming PGM with the addition of a P. Thus it has in some way ceased to be an act of Grand Lodge in 1766 but rather the act of a Past Grand Master.

---

introduce innovation and to seduce the brethren'. None of this however stopped lodges working the Royal Arch.

[36] Over the years there has been some confusion as to whether the Caledonian Chapter was changed into the Excellent Grand and Royal Chapter by Lord Blayney. Bernard Jones in the *Freemasons' Book of the Royal Arch* pp69-70 is adamant that this did not happen. He cites the first Minute Book of the Grand and Royal Chapter as running from March 1765 to December 1767; so it predates Lord Blayney's Exaltation by a good year. It seems that at this time the Chapter had no specific name but acquired the name in 1766. It is worth noting that this Chapter had in its Minute Book under the date of June 1765 a self-conferred Charter. Thus Blayney's Exaltation and the Charter of Compact were the culmination of a plan to give structure and an identity to the Royal Arch.

Whoever made the change of date clearly did not wish to see the Royal Arch have a direct and close association with the Moderns Grand Lodge. Lord Blayney's early masonic life is not known so one cannot know whether this rapid Exaltation in an English Chapter (which simply constituted itself to be Grand) was a repeat of an earlier Exaltation in the (Irish) military lodge of his Initiation, or whether it was a totally new degree to him.

In the preamble to the Charter Lord Blayney's honorifics are described as follows:

> We, the Right Honourable and Right Worshipful Cadwallader Lord Blayney of Monaghan in the Kingdom of Ireland, Lord Lieutenant and Custos Rotulorum on the same County and Major General in his Majesty's Service (P.) Grand Master of Free and Accepted Masons, And also Most Excellent Grand Master of the Royal Arch of Jerusalem.

It would seem that he was using his rank of Grand Master simply as one of his titles and that he was signing as Grand Master of the Royal Arch. However at the top of the Charter were three coats of Arms: the Royal Arms, those of Lord Blayney and also of the (Moderns) Grand Lodge itself. Was this act by Blayney merely a reflection of the interest of Modern masons in the Royal Arch or a part of his desire to see Antientness restored to the Moderns? Sadly we shall never know and clearly also the time was not yet right for any meeting of minds between the two streams of freemasonry.

No practical use was made of the Charter until late 1768 and the first warrants were sanctioned in January 1769. The Charter itself was renewed on 10th March 1769 by all those present signing. Samuel Spencer died in the middle of 1768 and thus one must be drawn to the conclusion that he personally was greatly disapproving of the Royal Arch.[37] Either way the Royal Arch clearly continued to remain outside the interests of the Moderns Grand Lodge, and only eventually achieved open acknowledgement in 1813 and a proper place in 1817.

---

[37] A concise article on this interesting episode is given by J R Dashwood in *AQC* Vol.64 pp136-7.

John Murray, 3rd Duke of Atholl (1729-1774)
Grand Master of England 1771-1774,
Grand Master of Scotland 1773-1774

Chapter 4 - Grand Lodge Animosities

It is probably correct that at first the Moderns Grand Lodge did not take the arrival of the Antients very seriously. However as the Antients continued to grow and prosper and especially when they came into 'constant correspondence' with Ireland and later Scotland to the exclusion of the Moderns it must have started to become clear to the Moderns that something had to be done.

The Antients had seized a marketing advantage with their branding, of both themselves and their competition. Indeed so effective was it that even 250 years later the appellations of Antient and Modern are used as shorthand for the two organisations. Their claim to represent the 'original' was a powerful one and hard for the Moderns to dispel, and their inclusion of the Royal Arch added extra value to their product. The Moderns had been used to the fact that, as Anderson implied, all lodges owed some sort of allegiance to the Grand Lodge in England.

Clearly the Moderns also started to experience more members practising the Royal Arch and responded in 1766 with a Grand Chapter. However when it came to what was going on overseas in the British Empire they must have felt very much at a disadvantage when they had to face the 'combined' numbers of Antient, Irish and Scottish military lodges.

The traditional tactic adopted by both sides to deal with those who changed allegiance was the practice of 'remaking'. There had been cases as early as 1730 of remakings of brothers of other Constitutions, especially Irish, but the practice became common following the rise of the Antients. Typically a brother would, after being tested, take the three degrees again and (of course) pay the necessary fees. Quite what was the necessary fee varied from the full fee to a simple couple of shillings before allowing him to join. Attitudes to this and to visiting varied and some lodges were more relaxed than others and it may be that increasing distance from London allowed for a less strict approach. This less strict approach was probably especially true because while Grand Lodge might have changed the order of the passwords and signs in the first two degrees that did not necessarily mean that all lodges changed their practises immediately nor that they had forgotten the original order.

In 1767 the Duke of Beaufort was elected Grand Master of the Moderns[38] and the following year reintroduced the idea of incorporating Freemasonry through a Royal Charter[39]. The first occasion was in 1763 under the Grandmastership of the Earl of Ferrers (1762-64). Thomas Edmondes, a Grand Warden, in an address dated November 1763 stated that the Earl of Ferrers proposed 'to set on foot the best approved plan to erect a proper building for the accommodation of the grand convocation, together with spacious rooms for a growing library, and school' and 'as soon as a freehold spot of ground or a convenient

---

[38] The sequence of Grand Masters was Earl Ferrers (1762-64), Lord Blayney (1764-67) and then the Duke of Beaufort (1767-68). Ferrers proposed the idea but failed to follow it through and then seemingly it must not have appealed to Lodge Blayney who followed him as Grand Master. The idea was then later taken up again with vigour by Beaufort.

[39] Ivor Grantham, 'The Attempted Incorporation of the Moderns', in *AQC* Vol.46 pp117-195 contains a long and exceptionally detailed account of the events relating to the Incorporation

building can be bought for the purpose, he will, at his own expence, use his utmost endeavours to get a charter, to make us a body corporate.'

What is being referred to is the creation of a legal entity, as opposed to a society composed of individuals, which is able to buy and sell property and pursue its agreed objectives in its own right. Maybe the Moderns wanted to be able to stand comparison with the old London Livery Companies, which even at this time were moving from functioning as controllers of trade to becoming more charitable in nature. Maybe part of this was to secure the hall they planned to construct or perhaps to be able to exercise some form of monopoly over all freemasons. Having read over two hundred pages of an article in AQC by Ivor Grantham[40] I remain unclear what the practical benefits were expected to be; for after all the society is still not incorporated and we have a headquarters and practice being freemasons some 250 years later. Matters such as disclosure of ritual might well have been an issue and for the purposes of this book any attempt to remove the Antients from the scene by the Moderns might have had a dramatic impact if it had succeeded. However it did not succeed.

The intentions of the Duke of Beaufort were unveiled at a meeting held at the Horn Tavern on 21st October 1768. As it is recorded he said incorporating the society would 'add to its Ancient dignity and lustre, as to establish its incomparable laws on a firm, solid and permanent basis'. The problem was initially that they did not have the funds to fulfil their grand plans for a hall and school. However they quickly compiled a list of eleven sets of charges that would be levied on lodges and brethren, which was computed to raise, by their estimates, the sum of £1290-1-0 on average each year. The year of 1769 was to bring challenges to the scheme, in particular from Caledonian Lodge No.325.

Among the long list of arguments advanced by Caledonian Lodge in February 1769 were:-

- That Incorporation was inappropriate to a Society composed of men of all trades and professions.

---

[40] *AQC* Vol.46 (1936) I Grantham 'The Attempted Incorporation of the Moderns' pp117-221.

- That Incorporation would necessitate the exposure of all masonic secrets.
- That Incorporation would result in members of foreign nationality acquiring rights and privileges in this country denied to foreigners.
- That an Incorporated Society quartered in London would possess no right to impose taxation upon Societies situated abroad.

The draft Charter of Incorporation only makes reference to the origins of the society as being 'originally instituted for humane and beneficent Purposes'. Towards the end of a long document comes the interesting sentence:

> And We do give and grant unto the said Grand Master, or his Deputy, his or their Successors for the Time being, full Power and Authority, by Virtue of these our Letters Patent, to issue Warrants for the constituting of subordinate Lodges; and the said Lodges, warranted as aforesaid, shall be, and they are hereby declared to be legal and regular.

The implication is that any lodge without a warrant from the incorporated society would be neither legal nor regular.

Forms were sent to all lodges to vote upon the proposition and by 28th April 1769 168 lodges had voted for and 43 against the proposition. These replies were those received in a four week period after the letters were sent out. At the time there were around 437 lodges on the register, of which over 390 had paid their dues. Either way the meeting decided that the proposition should be approved.

Determined opposition continued and while those lodges against the proposal were a minority, they were lodges of note, and they were determined to make their point and to be heard. At the end of May a meeting of the opposition prompted the Grand Secretary to issue a three page folio printed letter to all lodges on 12th July. By October there were further problems. A proposition was put that the funds of Grand Lodge, a total of some £1300, which it seems comprised the charity fund, should annually be transferred into the names of the Grand Officers of the year; this proposition met with strong opposition but the proposition passed. The sum was at the Bank of England and thus soundly invested and secure.

The Past Grand Treasurer and his two sureties declined to pass the funds over as they were being held for the benefit of the previous Grand

Officers – Lord Blayney, Col' Salter, Mr Ripley & Mr Tufnall the previous Grand Officers. The Grand Secretary Heseltine wrote to Lord Blayney on 29th November 1769 seeking his agreement to the transfer. On 23rd February 1770, pleading a 'tedious fitt of the gout' and the need to consult his fellow Obligees he declines on the grounds that these funds for charity would be appropriated to the expense of obtaining the Act of Incorporation. Somewhat later on 'May ye 10th-70' from Castle Blayney is a letter of capitulation from Lord Blayney, and the funds then got transferred.

While the petition to Parliament was drafted by February 1770 it was not actually presented until February 1772.[41] There were two readings on 28th February and 4th March 1772, followed by it being deferred for three months on 1st April. It is curious that this is the last heard of the Act of Incorporation. It did however come after a letter of 6th March to The Public Advertiser, signed HIRAM of which one section is well worth reciting:

> I have great Hopes that the House of Commons will so immediately perceive the Absurdity of this Scheme as to reject the Bill, otherwise they will entail upon themselves a vast Increase of Business, as I am told the Albions, Bucks and Antigallicans only wait the Issue of this Affair to petition for separate charters for themselves.

In the *London Evening Post* of 2nd April 1772 was a note:

> That the Free and Accepted Masons who had petitioned the House of Commons to incorporate them (finding the opposition to the bill which was brought in for that purpose to be too great for them to overcome) sheltered themselves yesterday (being *April Day*) from the ridicule they most naturally endured from a debate on the subject, by deferring the said bill for three months; their Deputy Grand Master, C.D. Esq.; at whose particular request it was so deferred, declaring it was his intent, by thus deferring it, to put it off *for ever*.

The Antients could not possibly have been unaware of these events and in *The Middlesex Journal* of mid April reporting a meeting of the Antients noted a letter from the Duke of Atholl for inviting him to

---

[41] It seems, as ever, that it is the lawyers who always make money. A bill from the firm of Allen and Rigge shows no activity on the matter of Incorporation between November 1770 and the end of January 1772. Their total bill came to £105

continue as Grand Master for another year which included '...he likewise acquainted them, that he was of opinion (and it is the opinion of the Society in general) that the MODERN MASONS are acting entirely inconsistent with the antient custom and principle of the craft'. This was rapidly denied in the next issue by the Grand Secretary, William Dickey.

The Moderns did proceed with their plan to build a hall for themselves. It was built in 1775 and opened the following year; thus there was some beneficial outcome to events. Great Queen Street has furnished the home of English freemasonry for almost 250 years.

The Antients had matters to be pleased with. In 1771 they elected the 3rd Duke of Atholl as Grand Master and he served until his death on 5th November 1774. Perhaps rather more to the point was that in November 1773 he was also elected as Grand Master Mason of the Grand Lodge of Scotland, and was thus Grand Master both north and south of the border. At the meeting of the Antients on 2nd September 1772 they resolved to establish constant correspondence with both Ireland and Scotland[42]. Ireland agreed on 5th November 1772 and Scotland on 30th November 1772 (this also being the meeting where the Duke became Grand Master Elect). As Scotland's letter to England stated:

> ...he to assure the Right Worshipful Grand Lodge of England, in the most respectful manner, of the desire which the Grand Lodge of Scotland has to cultivate a connection with them, by a regular correspondence, for the interest of the Ancient Craft, suitable to the honour and dignity of both Grand Lodges.

And with that agreement in place the Duke of Atholl could happily be Grand Master in both places and in correspondence with Ireland as well. The Moderns were left totally excluded by the agreement between the three Grand Lodges. Possibly they needed some time to consider alternative strategies.

---

[42] This was the first occasion of a concerted cooperation between the three Grand Lodges and was conducted purely by mail between the Grand Secretaries. In many ways this marks the start of a very much closer relationship between the Home Grand Lodges than had existed before.

William Preston (1742-1818) Freemason, Educator,
Author of Illustrations of Masonry

Chapter 5 - Wm Preston's 'Diplomatic' Initiative

The arrival of the Dukes of Atholl on both the English and Scottish masonic scenes seems to mark a change in the previously acrimonious relationship, or perhaps non-relationship, between the Moderns and Antients. The 3rd Duke of Atholl (1729-1774) became Grand Master of the Antients in 1771 and continued until his death on 5th November 1774, and in November 1773 had also become Grand Master Mason in Scotland. In spite of his untimely death this must have publicly established the closeness between the Antients and Scotland. The new 4th Duke of Atholl (1755-1830) was only 19 at this time but the Antients decided, and he accepted, that he should be the new Grand Master. Accordingly on 25th February 1775 in the Grand Masters Lodge No.1 he received his three degrees and following 'appropriate instruction' he became Master of the lodge the same day. He was elected Grand Master on 1st March and formally installed on the 25th of March. Thus the Antient-Scottish bond through the Dukes of Atholl was maintained.

The Moderns had their own preoccupations, and indeed for many years they had desired a suitable home to match their aspirations in society. In 1775 the cornerstone was laid for the Freemasons Hall in Great Queen Street in London and the new building, the first purpose built hall to house a Grand Lodge, was opened the following year. It was later complemented by the building of a Freemasons Tavern in 1786. With the thoughts of both parties focused elsewhere one might have expected some sort of truce. Nobody however had bargained for the intervention of William Preston in 1775.

William Preston[43] is a name to be conjured with, not only in England, but worldwide because he remains known to this day for his *Illustrations of Freemasonry* and the legacy of the Prestonian Lectures[44]. He was an interesting character, indeed a man of outstanding knowledge and strong opinions. William Preston was born in Edinburgh on 7th August 1742 and died in London on 1st April 1818. His father had died when William was a teenager and as a result William had to leave college finding a job first as a secretary and later as a printer. In 1760 he left for London and secured a job with William Strahan, the King's Printer, a job he kept for many years.

He was initiated into freemasonry in 1763 in an Antients lodge. He and a group of Scottish expatriates had hoped to establish a lodge under the Grand Lodge of Scotland in London but they soon found their application refused and they were recommended to approach the Antient

---

[43] Colin Dyer in 1987 produced a full biography entitled *William Preston and His Work* (published by Lewis Masonic. ISBN 0-85318-149-7) and while now out of print can be obtained secondhand.

[44] The practice of Prestonian lectures fell into decay and was later revived as detailed in the Extract from the Grand Lodge Proceedings for December 5th, 1923.
'In the year 1818, Bro. William Preston, a very active Freemason at the end of the eighteenth and beginning of the nineteenth centuries, bequeathed £300 of 3 per cent. Consolidated Bank Annuities, the interest of which was to be applied 'to some well-informed Mason to deliver annually a lecture......for a number of years the terms of this bequest were acted upon, but for a long period no such Lecture has been delivered, and the Fund has gradually accumulated, and is now vested in the M.W. the Pro. Grand Master, the Rt. Hon. Lord Ampthill, and W. Bro. Sir Kynaston Studd, P.G.D., as trustees. The Board has had under consideration for some period the desirability of framing a scheme which would enable the Fund to be used to the best advantage; and, in consultation with the Trustees who have given their assent, has now adopted such a scheme... and will be put into operation when the sanction of Grand Lodge has been received.' So thus was revived the tradition of the Prestonian Lecture.

Grand Lodge in London, which it seems on 2nd March 1763 granted them a dispensation to start a lodge.[45] The lodge was granted the number 111 and William Preston was their second candidate. All did not go well for in 1764 it seemed that the members of the lodge had decided to switch their allegiance to the Moderns and as Stephen Jones[46] says Preston and others 'prevailed on the rest of the lodge at the Half Moon Tavern to petition for a Constitution. Lord Blayney, at that time Grand Master, readily acquiesced with the desire of the Brethren, and the lodge was soon after constituted a second time…as the Caledonian Lodge'. Alas why they chose to make this move is not known and there are no clues in the archives. By 1768 Preston was no longer a member of Caledonian Lodge. He had been busy discovering the variety of freemasonry and of publishing the first edition of his *Illustrations of Freemasonry* in 1772 followed by a second one in 1774.

The Lodge of Antiquity No.1 was in a bad way in 1774 having very few active members. At a meeting in March they passed a motion to cancel the previous requirement of charging every Mason half a guinea for admission, immediately after which Bro. Noorthouck proposed Bro. Preston for membership. On the surface it seemed that the Lodge of Antiquity was flourishing with more members, but the changes that Preston was introducing did not meet with the approval of all the members and it seems that some of the candidates brought in by Preston were disruptive.

Matters came to a head in December 1777 when the chaplain of the lodge offered to preach a sermon on St Johns Day, 27th December. This was to be done at St Dunstan's Church in Fleet Street, to a congregation of the Master and members of the lodge. Quite how the members were to

---

[45] While this practise no longer occurs in Britain it does still occur in North America where it is normal for a new lodge to start with its name but instead of a number simply the letters UD after. The new lodge being 'Under Dispensation' does all the things that a lodge does and normally after a year there is a formal proceedings by which the lodge is then Constituted. Under the English Constitution today a lodge may do nothing until it is Consecrated. This is one occasion where the Antients practice did not get adopted after the Union while the practice continued unchanged in North America.

[46] Stephen Jones was a close friend of William Preston and was the author of the *'Memoirs of Mr William Preston'* which was published in the January 1795 edition of the *Freemasons Magazine*.

get from the Mitre Tavern to St Dunstan's was unclear. Bro Noorthouck sent apologies for his absence and at the same time enquiring "how far the Master was authorised to lead out his Lodge in a Masonic manner". In the event the lodge walked in procession wearing regalia to the church. There followed an argument on the propriety of doing this, and of the rights of the lodge to take this action, which led eventually to the whole matter of processing being discussed in Grand Lodge in February 1778. In the end Preston was not willing to compromise and he and nine others were expelled from freemasonry.

On 17th July 1778 one Jacob Bussey was a visitor at the Lodge of Antiquity. Bussey was the Grand Secretary of the old Lodge at York – which styled itself The Grand Lodge of All England. There were exchanges of letters while positions were sorted out and the desire of the renegade members of the Lodge of Antiquity eventually became clear. A letter from one Benjamin Bradley to York of 22nd September 1778 reads:

> …A Warrant or Deputation from York to a few members of the R.W. Lodge of Antiquity to Act as a Grand Lodge for that Part of England South of the Trent, with a Power to Constitute Lodges in that Division, when properly applied for, and a regular Correspondence to be kept up, and some token of Allegiance to be annually given on the part of the Brethren thus Authorised to Act.[47]

Thus there became two Lodges of Antiquity. In November 1778, on an evening when both lodges were holding meetings at the Mitre, that part still with the Moderns Grand Lodge sent a note to the 'Preston contingent' demanding that the property of the lodge should be handed back. Upon reading this note they decided to move their next meeting to the Queen's Arms and left that evening taking with them all the lodge property in three or four coaches. However it was not until 24th June

---

[47] The exchanges of letters are all printed in detail in Colin Dyers book *William Preston and his Work* for those wishing a blow by blow account. This letter is on page 66. The mere survival of the correspondence gives a lively insight into the generally less structured nature of freemasonry in England at the time. One can reflect that the habit of taking a warrant from another body to constitute another Grand body appears elsewhere in the book and is a practice still used to this day as a means of creating a new Grand Masonic order. The success of such breakaways would not seem to be particularly high.

1779 that they were ready to hold the first meeting of their new Grand Lodge, The Grand Lodge of England South of the River Trent[48].

This intransigence and what followed is perhaps indicative of the sometimes impetuous nature of William Preston as a man and offers valuable background to the earlier incident of 1775 which involved the Grand Lodge of Scotland.

Preston, then a Modern mason for just over a year, had written to the Grand Secretary of the Grand Lodge of Scotland on 7th August seeking information for inclusion in his *Freemasons Calendar*[49].

> I take the liberty in the Character of a Mason to apply to you for a correct list of the present Officers of the Grand Lodge of Scotland of the several lodges of your Constitution. As it is intended for an Annual Publication which goes to press about a month hence I should be greatly obliged if favour'd with an Answer from you by return of Post. Any expence that may attend this favour shall be cheerfully paid to any of your Correspondents in London.

However the dynamite was in the postscript of the letter

> I should be extremely happy to be Instrumental in introducing a Correspondence between the Grand Lodge of Scotland, the place of my Nativity, And the Grand Lodge of England, my Interest and Connexions in Masonry are at present very extensive here, and it would give me a sensible pleasure to have the Satisfaction of Recommending English Brethren to

---

[48] This Grand Lodge only warranted two new lodges in ten years and in 1789 Preston and the other members who were expelled with him made their peace with the Moderns Grand Lodge and rejoined the Lodge of Antiquity.

[49] The names and meeting places of lodges were recorded in the Engraved List of Lodges published by the Moderns Grand Lodge annually. William Preston decided to produce a Freemasons Calendar through the Stationers Company, who claimed a monopoly over such almanacs. The first edition in 1775 did not meet with the approval of Grand Lodge for in November of 1775 that matter was raised, the Grand Secretary observing that "such Calendar was in many respects incorrect, and therefore a dishonour to the Society". Preston was asked to represent Grand Lodge and, perhaps not surprisingly, little progress was made. Grand Lodge considered they were entitled to some consideration from the Stationers, but nothing was forthcoming. They decided to publish the 1777 edition through a number of booksellers; the reality was that the previous monopoly had already been broken by a legal court case. It was after this episode that Preston's relationships with members of Grand Lodge started to deteriorate.

your favour, and the Brethren Initiated by you to the Regular Lodges of this Metropolis

William Masson, the Scottish Grand Secretary forwarded a copy to William Dickey, the Secretary of the Antients, and awaited his response before writing to Preston. When it came the response to Preston was firm and to the point.

> …as the Grand Lodge of Scotland have an Establish'd Correspondence with the Grand Lodges of England and Ireland, and they the same with us, whatever new matter happens with the One is made known to all, so I made this known to my worthy Brother Dickey Secretary of the Grand Lodge of England, and of him in Bow Street, Covent Garden you will get any Information you want to publish with regard to Masonry.

Preston was not so easily put off and on 3rd October 1775 replied at length and with his usual considerable vigour. It is worth quoting at length because it demonstrates the ill-will felt by Preston, which was presumably some mirror of that felt by the Moderns for the Antients at that time, and the distance that had to be travelled in reaching an eventual accommodation.

> Yours of the 7th Ult. I received, and am much obliged for your recommendation to Mr Dickey, whom you style Secretary of the Grand Lodge of England, for ye intelligence relative to the fraternity in Scotland. I have not the pleasure of knowing that Gentleman, nor do I wish to correspond with him in the Character you give him. It is with regret I understand by your Letter that the Grand Lodge of Scotland has been so grossly imposed upon, as to have establish'd a Correspondence with an irregular body of men who falsely assume the appellation of *Antient Masons*, and I still more sensibly lament that the imposition has likewise received the Countenance of the Grand Lodge of Ireland. The limits of a letter will not enable me so fully to explain this matter as I could wish; for your information I therefore inclose parts of the History of Masonry in England from the revival of the Grand Lodge in 1717. In the perusal of this history in the years 1736, 37, 38 and 39 you will find the Origin of these irregular Masons with whom you correspond. On the Authenticity of the particulars you may depend and from the list of Grand Masters from 1717 to the present time which I likewise enclose you will find a regular chain of succession observed for 15 years after the revival of the Grand Lodge here, the Quarterly Communications are regularly enter'd and subscribed by the different Noblemen who presided over the Society. This is the best authority I can produce to convince you that our Society is the only Antient and

respectable Body of Masons, And that the other Masons here who falsely assume the Appellation have no such Vouchers to produce and are of too recent a date and of too unconstitutional an Origin to Merit the favour or patronage of either the Grand Lodge of Scotland or Ireland. <u>I am sorry to find that the Duke of Athol, Genl. Oughton, Lord Kellie and some other respectable personages have at various times been prevailed upon to give a Sanction to those Assemblies. I am convinced no Nobleman, apprised of the deception, would give them countenance</u>, (author's underlining) or wish to Intrude on the rights of the Noblemen who ever since the year 1721 have been regularly elected to preside as Grand Masters agreeable to the Antient Laws of the Society. You will find by the lists that the greater part of our patrons have been Noblemen of Scotch Extraction who have regularly attained to the direction of the fraternity. Under our patronage 480 lodges are established at home and abroad and some of the first Princes in Europe do not disdain our Alliance. Such is the true State of our Society here, and I hope the information I transmit will at least excite your curiosity to enquire more Minutely into the Affair.

The underlined sentence in Preston's letter, where he chooses to rubbish two Scots who had not only been Grand Masters of the Antients but also Grand Masters in Scotland as well, perhaps points us to William Preston's greatest weakness. For him to consider that he might gain a sympathetic ear in Edinburgh by maligning two Past Grand Master Masons of Scotland would seem to indicate a political naivety on his part.

When we look at Preston's *Illustrations of Masonry* we do need to remember that the first two editions (1772 and 1774) are from when he was an Antient mason, and from 1774 to 1778 as a Modern Mason, then until 1789 in the equivocal position of being involved in The Grand Lodge South of the River Trent, before being back in the bosom of Modern masonry once again. It speaks volumes for his independent mind and determination that he was able to change allegiances so often and yet still be welcomed back. One might perhaps view his intervention with Scotland on behalf of the Moderns as an act that was very much in character, even if lacking in accuracy and any sense of strategic direction. In reality it changed nothing but at the time was well documented and so must have been considered some sort of threat. It was perhaps the last outburst during the period during which the 4th Duke of Atholl was Grand Master of the Antients and there is little more to report until the first moves towards Union.

John, 4th Duke of Atholl, Grand Master (Antients)1775-1781 and 1791-1813, Grand Master (Scotland) 1778-1780

Chapter 6 - Revolutions, Unrest and the Unlawful Societies Act of 1799

The American War of Independence or American Revolutionary War of 1775-83 between the thirteen states and Great Britain, which resulted in the loss of the American colonies, was a shock to the British establishment. France joined in the war in 1778, and so later did both Spain and the Dutch Republic. The French participation in the war drove the country near to bankruptcy and ruined the French economy. Perhaps even more importantly there was a much greater awareness of radical ideas regarding governance, participation in government and religious tolerance circulating in society.

France's dire financial position, which it could not manage, was compounded by rising food prices following bad harvests[50] and a general

---

[50] It seems these poor harvests, perhaps a final straw for the French populace, were due to a combination of El Nino and volcanic eruptions of the Laki and Grimsvoten volcanoes in Iceland.

resentment against aristocracy and privilege. In 1789 matters came to a head and the Bastille was stormed, setting in train a tide of revolutionary activity, the French Revolution, which lasted till 1799. This gave rise to a set of ideas that would sweep across Europe

Perhaps inspired by events in France, the Society of United Irishmen was formed in 1791. Its secretary, the Dublin Protestant lawyer, Wolfe Tone, wanted to convince the Protestant dissenters that they and the Roman Catholics shared the need for Parliamentary reform. By 1794 this stance had changed to one of seeking a break with Britain and the establishment of a republic. Contact with the French to gain assistance led to a French fleet with 15,000 troops setting sail. They were scattered by storms and a landing at Bantry Bay was abandoned. In 1797 there was a financial crisis, an end to subsidies on grain and the new war taxes were biting hard. Finally in May 1798 open rebellion broke out in Dublin. A small French force landed in Co Mayo and was captured. Over the year around 30,000 Irish lives were lost in the rebellion. At this time thoughts were also turning to Catholic Emancipation, which found less favour in the north of Ireland than in the South. It was known that there were branches of United Scotsmen and United Englishmen on the British mainland and incriminating evidence of United Irishmen was found among those participating in the naval mutinies of 1797 at Spithead and the Nore.

There was also developing intellectual pressure for changes in England: ideas were coming from France partly from Enlightenment thinking and also partly as a result of the French Revolution. The real risk however was probably as much from Englishmen as from France. Thomas Paine, radical propagandist and revolutionary, author of the *Rights of Man,* is one name still known today, whose views the government distrusted. As previously mentioned he had managed to be both in America and again in France for both revolutions. On the other side was Edmund Burke who had supported the American Revolution but later became opposed to the French Revolution. Other activist figures of note were people like the poets Samuel Taylor Coleridge and William Wordsworth, and scientist and Dissenter Joseph Priestley, all of whom could command an audience.

In such a febrile atmosphere we find one MP in a letter to the Home Office stating his willingness to assist 'in detecting the secret societies which may infest the parts around us'. With varying degrees of justification secret and seditious societies bound by oaths were seen as lurking round every corner and the government of Pitt the Younger decided, backed by public sentiment, that stricter control was required. Accordingly it introduced 'An Act for the more effectual suppression of societies established for seditious and treasonable purposes; and for the better preventing treasonable and seditious practices' – the act we know today as *The Unlawful Societies Act 1799*. While the 1798 rebellion in Ireland had been defeated, the real strength of the United Irishmen, Scotsmen and Englishmen was not really known. Pitt was accused in Parliament of exaggerating the dangers but stated that the risks could be proved and he set up a Parliamentary committee to examine the evidence. When reporting back they had found, perhaps not surprisingly, evidence of danger, the greatest risk lying in 'the institution of political societies, of a nature and description before unknown in any country, and inconsistent with public tranquillity and with the existence of public government'. Within a month of this report the government set out its proposals. As well as those societies already suspected (those with 'wicked and illegal engagements of mutual fidelity and secrecy by which the members are bound') it was proposed that 'all societies which administer such oaths shall be declared unlawful confederacies' would also be included in the Bill.

Quite clearly freemasonry fell within the scope of this definition. Escaping from closure under the act would, for example, require initiations to be done in public, and for a list of members to be maintained open for inspection. Both points could well prove hard to achieve in practice. A few days after the second reading of the bill, on the 2nd May 1799, a delegation of freemasons went to meet Pitt, the Prime Minister, at Downing Street. They included the Earl of Moira, Acting Grand Master of the Moderns, the Duke of Atholl, Grand Master of the Antients and Past Grand Master Mason of Scotland and other senior masons. The Minutes of the Hall Committee records the views expressed by Pitt:

> The delegation reported back that the Prime Minister had 'expressed his good opinion of the Society and said he was willing to recommend any Clause to prevent the New Act from affecting the Society, provided that the

Name of the Society could be prevented of being made use of as a Cover by evilly disposed persons for Seditious purposes'[51].

This could have been no easy meeting. Through the Earl of Moira one can almost feel the weight of his commitment given when in 1808 he subsequently recalled his words of that day.

I have pledged myself to His Majesty's ministers that should any set of men attempt to meet as a lodge without sanction, the Grand Master, or Acting Grand Master (whomsoever he might be), would apprise parliament.[52]

On 6th May Pitt introduced the clauses exempting freemasonry from the Act. It received its third reading in the House of Commons and the bill passed over to the House of Lords[53]. The final debate took place on 20th June and the first speaker was the Earl of Radnor[54] who desired to

---

[51] J M Hamill. *The Earl of Moira, Acting Grand Master 1790-1813* in *AQC* Vol.93 p47

[52] The letter in which Moira made this declaration is printed in full in David Murray Lyon, *History of the Lodge of Edinburgh embracing an account of the Rise and Progress of Freemasonry in Scotland* (Edinburgh and London: William Blackwood, 1873), p. 266. Note: This reference appears on p293 in the 1900 edition.

[53] It is one of those quirks that Colonel Fullarton, MP for Ayrshire and not a mason, received a petition from Mother Kilwinning (see under) asking him to inform the Prime Minister that they existed and also wished to be exempted from the terms of the Act. The outcome was that the original clauses in the bill were amended to remove any references to Grand Lodges or their authority and gave immunity simply to all lodges which had existed before the passing of the Act. Authority was something sought by the Grand Lodges and from 1800 The Grand Lodge of Scotland insisted that Scottish lodges which did not send their returns to Grand Lodge (with the annual dues!) would fall outside the exemptions within the Act.
Mother Kilwinning is a lodge in Ayrshire whose origins the Grand Lodge of Scotland today describes as 'before 1598'. The issue was one of precedence in the roll of Grand Lodge and The Lodge of Edinburgh came to be at the top of the list. Kilwinning had reservations about this and on failing to get promoted to the top of the list quietly left Grand Lodge in 1743. It acted as a Grand Lodge, chartering daughter lodges, until its return to Grand Lodge in 1813. Thus its claim in 1799, submitted through its MP, was a valid one.

[54] A report of this debate is in *The Senator* Vol.23 (1799) pp1728-32 and is used here. The Earl of Radnor is described in *The Vision, Liber Veritatis* by William Beckford Vol.5 p127 as 'queer looking punctilious…that Grand Borer after forms and precedents in the House of Lords and Dictator at Quarter Sessions and Turnpike meetings, by way of relaxation in the Country…cross-grained, close fisted and a notorious driver of hard bargains…'. A full account of events surrounding the Act can be read in *The Unlawful Societies Act of 1799* by Andrew Prescott. It is in *The Canonbury Papers I* (2002) pp116-134 and also freely online.

see the exemption for freemasons dropped from the Bill. He was reported thus:

> Not himself being a mason, and having heard that they administered oaths of secrecy, he did not know, whether in times so critical as the present, it was wise to trust the freemasons any more than other meetings'.

The Duke of Atholl responded in defence of the institution of freemasonry:

> The Noble Duke contended, that the imputations thrown upon freemasons by the Noble Earl, on the authority of a recent publication, however justified by the conduct of the lodges on the continent, were by no means applicable to those of Great Britain. His Grace avowed, that the proceedings in masonic lodges, and all their obligation to secrecy simply related to their own peculiar little tenets and matters of form. There were no set of men in the kingdom, and he had the best opportunities of knowing, having had the honour to preside over a great part of them in England as well as in Scotland, who could possibly be more loyal or attached to the person of their sovereign or the cause of their country. There was nothing in the masonic institution hostile to the law, the religion or the established government of the country; on the contrary, they went to support all these, and no person who was not a loyal or religious man could be a good mason. Of those well established facts perhaps the Noble Earl was ignorant in consequence of his not being a mason, but they were strictly true: added to these considerations, the masonic system was founded on the most exalted system of benevolence, morals, and charity, and many thousands were annually relieved by the charitable benevolence of masons. These very laudable and useful charities must necessarily be quashed did the bill pass into a law, as recommended by the Noble Earl. The very nature and foundation of freemasonry involved in them the most unshaken attachment to religion, unsuspected loyalty to sovereigns, and the practice of morality and benevolence, in the strictest sense of the words. To such regulations as went to prevent the perversion of their institution to the purposes of seditious conspiracy, he could have no objection, and as a proof of the readiness with which they would be acceded to by the masonic societies, he need only mention that this subject had occupied their attention for several years past...

The main result of this law was that lodges had to make annual returns which had to be lodged with the local Justices of the Peace (magistrates)[55].

---

[55] In Scotland Grand Lodge seized the opportunity to regulate its Daughter Lodges more closely and from 1799 the Register of Initiates (a physical volume solely for that

This practice fell into disuse over the years and, for example, Grand Lodge sent out a reminder to lodge secretaries in 1920 to remind them to make returns. Little enforced laws do remain laws and it is a curious reminder of this that in 1939 a Clerk of the Peace in Essex wrote to lodges telling them that only lodges founded before 1799 were entitled to exemption. This caused quite a ripple at the time, legal advice was taken and Counsel was of the opinion that this was a correct interpretation of the law. Grand Lodge tried to bring a private bill to correct this matter. In this period, just before the outbreak of World War II, times were troubled and the government declined to remove the offending clause but agreed not to prosecute any masonic lodges. The last remaining powers of the Unlawful Societies Act of 1799[56] were finally repealed in Section 13 (2) of the 1967 Criminal Law Act.

Perhaps most importantly this Act brought together the Moderns and Antients in common cause and the Earl of Moira and the Duke of Atholl both found it to their and freemasonry's advantage to cooperate. They were each able to express this in strong statements reflecting upon the honour of freemasonry in general, rather than just their own Grand Lodge. Perhaps this co-operation was a key moment in sparking thoughts of seeking a unity among English freemasonry that had been absent for over half a century?

---

purpose) shows increasingly improving data records for membership registrations. Also the Grand Lodge of Scotland required that its Lodges obtain annually a certificate to confirm that they had met the requirements of the Act in reporting names of members to the appropriate authorities otherwise Grand Lodge would not 'vouch' for the Lodge concerned: it would therefore have been deemed illegal and would have been forced to close. As an attempt to ensure that annual dues (known as test fees) were paid this effected only a partial success but it was some progress.

[56] The 1799 Act did not apply to Ireland but only to Great Britain as then defined. Two decades later the tense situation in Ireland in the 1820s had led to the suspension of the Habeas Corpus Act and prompted the 1823 Act for Preventing and Administering of Oaths. This was aimed at bodies such as the Orange Order and Ribbonmen, but just as in Britain in 1799 freemasonry got swept up in events. It failed to get a similar exemption before the Bill was enacted and it was some two years before this was achieved. Grand Lodge did not meet, many lodges closed never to reopen, and abroad Irish lodges did not know what their legal position was. This was a sad era which decimated freemasonry in Ireland.

Section of a letter from John Boardman DGT GL of Ireland to Thomas Harper DGM Antients, England dated 10th August 1805 regarding the Knights Templar order in Ireland.

Chapter 7 - Problems in Ireland

If one wants to understand the history of English masonry within Britain there is simply no escape from getting to grips with the story of Irish freemasonry. It was crucial as to how the Craft developed in England and, I will argue, actually changed the course of the freemasonry practised there today. One should never forget the close bonds between the Grand Lodges of the Antients, Ireland and Scotland before 1813 and especially the closer ones since the Union of 1813. It is not for nothing that they refer to themselves as the Three Home Grand Lodges. We should not be surprised at this because the national histories are similarly closely woven together and the British Empire was what the name implies and not just an 'English Empire'. In particular the regiments that were sent out around the world to make the Empire were often composed of a majority of non-English private soldiers and this explains how seemingly English regiments had Irish or Scottish military lodges attached to them. Such a melting pot also made the management of these lodges highly problematic as they travelled around the world. They also frequently had differences of opinion as they rubbed up against each other and local freemasonry. Given the number of military lodges working a form of masonry that was Antient in style it is not surprising that this predominates over the Moderns masonic style outside the United Kingdom.

Long standing unrest in Irish society turned into open rebellion in 1798, and an attempt to quieten the turmoil was sought by the British government. In 1799 the British House of Commons voted for Union while the Irish legislature rejected it. Opinions within Ireland were greatly divided, some were in favour of Catholic Emancipation, others favoured Union and others sought both Emancipation and Union. Eventually the Irish parliament accepted and in January 1801 Union came into force and the 'United Kingdom of Great Britain and Ireland' was established.

While the Grand Lodge of Ireland was established in 1725 there are no minutes until 1731, but from 1726 to 1731 minutes do exist for the Grand Lodge of Munster (that is to say the area round Cork). This Grand Lodge also contained a Time Immemorial Lodge known as Premier Lodge of Ireland No.1 Cork, a lodge believed to predate the Grand Lodge of Munster and which is still working to this day. It appears that Munster must have had the support of other lodges in the area because in 1728 it drew up rules for the guidance of lodges and unlike the Grand Lodge of Ireland retained its minutes. In 1731 Munster elected James 4th Earl of Kingston as Grand Master, he having already been installed as Grand Master in Dublin[57] – and thus ceased to be an independent entity. This demonstrates the point that in early days there could be more than one Grand Lodge in a 'territory' and this was also the case in England and Scotland.

The traumatic event in Irish masonic history of the first decade of the nineteenth century is often described by English masonic historians as the 'Seton Breakaway'. It is often mistold, because it was much more complicated than normally portrayed. These events were pivotal to the attempts to bring some order and structure to masonry. Before examining a series of letters from John Boardman, Grand Treasurer, in Dublin to

---

[57] Anyone wishing to research the masonic history of Ireland will soon discover the classic two volumes of the *History of the Grand Lodge of Ireland* consisting of Vol.1 by John Herron Lepper and Philip Crossle published by the Lodge of Research CC in 1925 and Vol.2 by R E Wilkinson in 1957. These are both out of print and only available as hard copies at extravagant prices. However digital copies are available for purchase from the librarian of the Grand Lodge of Ireland at a more realistic price.

Thomas Harper, Deputy Grand Master of the Antients in London[58], let us see who the correspondents are.

John Boardman, Grand Treasurer 1791-1814, was a Barrister-at-law in Dublin and came from an old Irish Quaker family. He remained in the post of Grand Treasurer and 'steered Grand Lodge safely through the two most critical periods of Irish Freemasonry, the Rebellion of 1798, and the Ulster Schism of 1805'[59]. Boardman was also a strong supporter of the Masonic Female Orphan School in Dublin for many years. Member of the Royal Dublin Society 1796-1814. Died in Chelsea, London on 29th May 1814.

Thomas Harper (circa 1735 –April 1832), came from humble origins. He was initiated in 1761 in Bristol, trained as a silversmith, and spent some time in Charleston, South Carolina. During the American Revolutionary War Harper was a Loyalist[60]. In 1785 he became Junior Grand Warden in the Antients Grand Lodge. As well as this he was a member of Globe Lodge No.23, the Lodge of Antiquity and other Moderns' lodges. It is perhaps a facet of his character that he managed to live this somewhat schizophrenic Masonic existence for a long time, in fact until 1803 when he was expelled from all his Moderns lodges. This was rescinded in 1810, perhaps when the value of his having had a foot in each camp became duly appreciated. In 1801, on the death of the Deputy Grand Master, William Dickey, he took on that role in the Antients. He

---

[58] By chance one leg of a series of letters exchanged between these two brothers was kept, the letters received by Thomas Harper. These are in the Library and Museum of Freemasonry in London in a file labelled 'Ireland Miscellaneous Correspondence' Ref. GBR 1991 HC 15/A/1-64. They do serve perfectly to illustrate the closeness of the relationship between the Antients and the Grand Lodge of Ireland.

[59] The comments of Dr Chetwode Crawley in Lepper and Crossle, 'History of the Grand Lodge of Ireland', Vol.1, p432. A brother from the North of Ireland might not express such sympathetic sentiments, but the role played by Boardman is undoubtedly significant.

[60] There was a tendency that the strength of the Moderns in America was south of the York River in the States where the economy was largely based on agriculture and plantations while the northern stated tended towards rather more Ancient masonry. During the American Revolutionary War (or American War of Independence) (1775-1783) the southern States were more strongly Loyalist while the north was more revolutionary. This may possibly explain the foot in both masonic camps that was maintained by Harper.

was one of the assessors who prepared the articles of Union and was a signatory to it in 1813. Harper remained a regular attendee at Grand Lodge until his death. By profession he was a silversmith of note and perhaps his greatest legacy to freemasonry is his Masonic jewels.

In a letter of 21st March 1801 to Thomas Harper, John Boardman writes from Dublin[61];

> A friend of mine Mr Graham who goes to London on business has kindly undertaken the delivery of this. I beg to introduce him to you as a very worthy and experienced mason and the Master of a respectable Lodge (No.36) in this city.
>
> Since our common and esteemed friend Mr Agar has been out of office as Deputy Grand Master I have not had the opportunity of being apprised of the proceedings of the Grand Lodge of England or the general concern of Masons in that Kingdom – I shall therefore if I do not (cause) too much trouble, entrust the favour of ( ) to transmit to me by Mr Graham such of those details as are usually printed for the information of the Craft for the last four or five years.
>
> I fancy no work of merit on the subject of masonry has been published since Preston's last edition. But if I am in error you will please to set me right on the head.
>
> I find you have incorporated Royal Arch with the Blue masonry, and sanctioned it under the authority of Grand Lodge. – here the case is different, & the Grand Lodge of Ireland only recognises the first three degrees. I wish to follow your example & engraft the fourth under the authority of the G.L. but before any measure can be taken for this purpose it is necessary to know whether separate warrants are granted by you for holding R.A. Chapters & what charge is made on issuing these. As I am anxious that the proceedings in both Kingdoms should correspond as nearly as possible I beg the favour of you to give me such information as may most likely point out the means of obtaining this desirable end.
>
> (and after his signature a question) Pray can you inform me whence the term Harodim is derived – is it the name of a person or a place and why applied to a chapter of the R.A.?

The correspondence draws to our attention that in addition to the formal interchange of letters there was also a personal one between senior officers in the Grand Lodges and at yet another level it also illustrates that

---

[61] Letter Ref GBR 1991 HC 15/A/2

John Boardman had a lack of familiarity with the form and structure of the Antients.

In Ireland the matter of the Royal Arch had been progressing and the matter of the Knights Templar had been added, for in a long letter dated 10th August 1805 John Boardman writes[62]:

> ...in order to obtain your advice and assistance upon some Masonic affairs now under theconsideration of our Grand Lodge. The Royal Arch has not been recognised or under the organisation of the Grand Lodge of Ireland – hence much irregularities have arisen, to remedy which a committee have been appointed, to propose necessary rules and regulations, preliminary to the Grand Lodge taking that degree under its protection and granting warrants &c therein...
>
> We have another degree, styled Knights templars which is very prevalent among the lower kind of masons and military lodges throughout the Kingdom – who act wholly independent of the Grand Lodge – obtain warrants & are registered &c by persons wholly unauthorised but who assume a pretended power of doing so - nay warrants for Knights templar degree have come to my hands, under the signature of persons, who were suspended from masonry by order of the Grand Lodge for gross misconduct – to put a stop to many evils which have arisen and are likely to arise from such proceedings – it has been submitted to take this degree under the cognizance of the Grand – not only as a measure of regulation but also of finance, for I think that the funds of the order will derive near £500 by it. Now I wish to know if your Grand Lodge recognises in any respect the degree of Knights templars – or if such a degree is even known to you, & whether you have any and what powers (save those given by the late Act of Parliament under which I conceive all irregular meetings of Masons or persons styling themselves such may be effectually proposed) by which you can check control or regulate disorders and irregularities committed in this degree?

The comment by Boardman upon the popularity of the Knights Templar among 'the lower kind of masons and military lodges throughout the Kingdom' gives a fascinating insight. One has to accept that this was from a member of the elite in Dublin, but nonetheless the comment being unprompted and in a private letter has a ring of reality to it. While there was clearly an attempt to bring some order to the structure of Irish freemasonry there was one other pervading and urgent need - a

---

[62] HC-15-A-9 Library and Museum of Freemasonry, London

financial one. In this case the thought of a much needed extra £500 of income per annum. In Ireland, as in Scotland, managing to prise the annual dues out of lodges was a major task with the lodges preferring to have the monies in their account rather than in Grand Lodge's.

However matters were already far advanced in Dublin for resolutions were passed in Grand Lodge on 5th September 1805 which created both a Grand Royal Arch Chapter and a Grand Knights Templars Encampment. There were several 'innovations' that were to resurface later in England. No person was to be initiated a Royal Arch Mason unless he was already a duly registered Master Mason; or admitted a Knight Templar unless being a Royal Arch Mason duly registered. Both bodies would be 'at all times regulating its proceedings, as much as possible, in conformity with the rules and regulations of the Grand Lodge'. On 19th September a note from John Leech G.S. – R.A.C.[63] notes that memorials from 11 lodges, all in Dublin, were read and granted to hold Royal Arch Chapters. At the same time it was resolved that 'a return of all Warrants granted for holding a Royal Arch Chapter be made to the Grand Lodge, specifying the Number of the Lodge to which each Royal Arch Warrant is attached'. The same clause relating to the Knights Templars did not have any requirement for a link relating it to a lodge. The 26th September 1805 also saw a warrant granted to Brothers Jaffray, Boardman, Leech (respectively Deputy Grand Master, Treasurer and Secretary of Grand Lodge), jointly with others for an Encampment and for a committee 'to regulate the proceedings and inspect the conduct of all Encampments held under the sanction and authority of the Grand Encampment'.[64]

These organisations, created by a Grand Lodge meeting composed of (solely) Craft masons, and without any involvement of those currently in either Royal Arch Chapters or the Early Grand Encampment was going to set the scene for an explosion of anger among the freemasonic

---

[63] John Leech signs himself G.S. R.A.C. While he was Grand Secretary (G.S) of the Grand Lodge in this instance the was Grand Secretary (G.S.) of the Royal Arch Chapter (R.A.C.).

[64] These manuscript notes are in the records of the Grand Lodge of Ireland and are taken from the CD published by the Grand Lodge of Ireland *No Taxation without Representation: The 'Revolution' of the Ulster Brethren'* and subtitled *'or Alexander Seton DGS and the Grand Lodge of Ulster v Alexander Jaffray DGS and John Boardman GT and the Establishment'*.

community. This crisis might have been a soluble problem if other factors had not been already present as irritants. Those which had been festering away behind the scenes were the under-representation of Ulster masons in Grand Lodge, and the problems of travelling to Dublin for meetings. The remuneration of Deputy Grand Secretaries and Deputy Grand Treasurers was in part by giving them a percentage of the monies collected – a matter that caused much ire among brethren. Combined with the appointment of a 'Northern' as Deputy Grand Secretary, this set the scene for rebellion – one that was to last until 1814!

1ˢᵗ Earl of Donoughmore (1767-1825)
GM Grand Lodge of Ireland (1789-1813)

Chapter 8 - More problems in Ireland

One might well ask why Ireland deserves two whole chapters in a book which is all about English freemasonry, and it is a fair question. The reality is that events in Ireland were no more distant to England then than they were a few decades ago. The previous chapter dealt with Irish attempts to bring order to an unstructured freemasonry. This chapter looks at just what happens when an insensitive minority ignores the hopes and aspirations of a large group of members. Given the brethren involved in the moves towards Union and their knowledge of these events in Ireland, and given the fractious nature of the populace across the whole of the United Kingdom and with the worries of the government about sedition and uprisings one would expect some caution. As these events unfold one has to wonder what the Duke of Sussex and Earl of Moira made of events in Ireland. Not only did they have to consider the risk of trouble from ordinary English masons if they felt that their values were being discarded by a Union of the two Grand Lodges but also how they would have to manage the other degrees.

My Irish story starts in 1801 with the 'Seton Breakaway' or 'Seton Sucession'. Gould does not even mention the event; and Pick and Knight deal with its start as follows:

> The story of this discreditable episode, which culminated in a violent struggle between two rival parties in Grand Lodge and eventually in the (temporary) formation of a separate Grand Lodge in Ulster, can be told quite simply.
>
> In 1801 D'Arcy Irvine, the Grand Secretary, had appointed as his deputy his friend, Alexander Seton, an able and energetic but dishonest barrister. This Seton was the villain of the piece. As soon as he was appointed, he went to the house of his predecessor and carried off a "hackney coach full" of books, MSS and other articles belonging to Grand Lodge some of which have never since been recovered.[65]

There is no mention in the Pick and Knight account of the attempts by the Grand Lodge of Ireland to bring the Royal Arch and Knights Templar into the fold. Seton is immediately cast by them as 'the villain of the piece', and his carrying off of a hackney coach full of books as a deliberate act of planned malice. What else, one might wonder, would a new Grand Secretary do but collect the papers of his predecessor? It is probably fair to consider this as the old view given to these events, and the Irish Lodge of Research CC's recent publications choose to portray events as a battle between North and South and between the Dublin establishment and the brethren outside. That is also my position but the whole story is a complex one and only an outline is in this chapter.

In 1796 George D'Arcy Irvine became Grand Secretary. He came from a masonic family; his father having been Provincial Deputy Grand Master of Masons in Ulster for many years. Grand Secretary was effectively an honorary post with most of the work being done by the Deputy Grand Secretary (DGS) to which post Irvine, in 1801, appointed one Alexander Seton, a barrister-at-law whose family came from Co. Tyrone in Ulster and were neighbours and friends of the D'Arcy family. Seton was assiduous in maintaining good relations with the lodges up in Tyrone and Fermanagh. Also typically the DGS was responsible for the collection of

---

[65] F L Pick & G N Knight, *The Pocket History of Freemasonry,* (1992) pp163-164. Sadly this excellent paperback size book is out of print but secondhand copies can often be found at fair prices online.

all the fees due to Grand Lodge. In return for that service he received, for example, 1 guinea for each warrant and 1s for every new member registered; 6d for every member transferred from one lodge to another; 1s for every Grand Lodge Certificate issued. Finally £10 "for his Trouble, care and Service" for every play organised by the Grand Lodge.

The Grand Treasurer was John Boardman. In 1801 Boardman announced that he had appointed William Semple as his deputy. Although the Grand Treasurer had this right it had not been exercised before but because of the infirmity of the previous DGS, Thomas Corker[66], the accounts were not in a good state and some £2000 had not been collected. Grand Lodge agreed and also fixed the remuneration of the Deputy Grand Treasurer at 50 guineas plus 10% commission on all arrears collected. It had of course been the job of the DGS to collect the monies and take a commission and Seton saw this as the removal of the perquisites of the job by Boardman. Semple resigned in 1803 and in his place Boardman appointed W F Graham.

Seton's good relations with the North led him to start collecting their dues, an activity that he believed was one of the DGS's tasks. Either way the relations between Seton and Boardman went from bad to worse and remained that way. It was against this background that the plan to take the Royal Arch and Knights Templar under the protection of Grand Lodge that caused the spark to ignite the tinder in 1806 and led to revolt. This was especially true because at the 1st May meeting of Grand Lodge D'Arcy Irvine was defeated in the vote for Grand Secretary. Seton waited outside the room in which the meeting had been held. When Boardman finally emerged Seton proceeded to publicly horsewhip him in front of the Brethren.

Open revolt was brewing. At the meeting of Grand Lodge on Thursday 5th June 1806 at 7pm a large number of unknown Brethren

---

[66] Thomas Corker became DGS in 1768 and kept the post until his death in 1801, a period of over 30 years. His name would have been synonymous with Grand Lodge as all communications would have been signed by him. A letter remains that he wrote to Laurence Dermott in September 1772 explaining how he came into the job and why he knew nothing of the previous agreement to be in constant correspondence with the Antients. The Antients must have felt he served them well for in 1783 he was presented with a gold medal 'as a token of esteem from the Grand Lodge of England. with the thanks of the Lodge for his many services and Brotherly Attention'.

appeared at the meeting. These were delegates who had come down from Ulster to demonstrate their displeasure. They rescinded a resolution passed against their submissions at a previous meeting and the resolutions regarding the Royal Arch and Knights Templar of the previous year were annulled. The Deputy Grand Master closed the meeting at 1am the next morning and left with the Grand Officers. The 'Northerns' remained, re-opened Grand Lodge and passed a whole host of resolutions only closing later that morning. From then till March 1808 there were two Masonic bodies in Dublin, both claiming to be Grand Lodge and both appealing to the Grand Master for his support. Boardman reported to Harper on 2nd November 1806[67] regarding the meeting:

> The infatuated and misguided Northerns acted as they pleased.

> The Grand Officers...requested the D Grand Master to decline any (subsequent) meeting of the Grand Lodge until his Lordships pleasure should be known – but as he has not as yet made any intimation on the subject...

> I presume to hope, you will treat all communications from such pretended Grand Lodge, or from Seton who still styles himself DG^d Secretary, tho dismissed from that office with the neglect and indifference they deserve.

Boardman had to wait a full year for any public support from England but on 2nd September 1807 it came from the Antients Grand Lodge:

> In consequence of certain Representations and official Documents having been transmitted from the RW Grand Lodge of Ireland to our RW Deputy Grand Master...

> That this R.W. Grand Lodge shall not, upon any Account, receive or acknowledge any Certificate issued by and under the Hand of said Alexander Seton, bearing Date at any Time subsequent to the 5th Day of June 1806... (and) neither shall any Person, by Virtue of such Certificate, be hereby received into any Lodge under the Sanction of this R.W. Grand Lodge, nor shall any such Person receive the Honours of Masonry among us.

The Grand Lodge of Ireland though wanted a little more, for in their address of thanks to the Antients dated 3rd December they wrote:

---

[67] The long letter of four full pages is in the Library and Museum of Freemasonry, London. Ref GBR 1991 HC 15/A/10.

The Grand Lodge of Ireland take the opportunity to express an anxious desire for a continuance of the cordial correspondence between the Grand Lodges of England and Ireland and offer their best regards and Brotherly good wishes for the welfare and happiness of the Brethren at large and for the prosperity of the Grand Lodge of England.

And perhaps they were wise to get this in place because Seton was active promoting the Grand East of Ulster[68]. For example in the Library and Museum of Freemasonry in London is a beautifully produced 'Memoire of certain transactions which occurred between the month of January 1806 and June 1808 in the Grand Lodge of Ireland'[69]. It is written in a fine hand, polite in tone, and elegantly bound with pale blue ribbon and sealed – and finally signed by one A. Seton! Its arrival in England failed to convince its readers.

The position of the Grand Master, the 1st Earl of Donoughmore, was complicated by his ill health, his presence on government business in London and being assailed with communications by both sides in the debate. In Ireland a series of long, acrimonious, and undoubtedly expensive law suits went to and fro. This included suits by the Grand Lodge of Ireland to recover their missing property – something they never achieved.

If anyone had the least doubt as to the seriousness of the revolt it must have been removed when representatives of 311 lodges met in Dungannon in 1808 and formed the Grand East of Ulster. Even allowing for some overstatement it was clear that the 'Northerns' were greatly dissatisfied with Grand Lodge in Dublin. There were however blows to come for the Grand East of Ulster.

---

[68] After the rebellious Grand Lodge meeting of 5th June 1806 there were for a time two bodies in Dublin, each calling themselves the Grand Lodge of Ireland, both appealing to the Grand Master and seeking support from brethren, lodges and other Grand Lodges. This situation continued until 1808. At the meeting of Grand Lodge held in May 1808 when it came to the election of the Grand Treasurer there was a call to check those voting against the registry of Warrants. Some of those voting came from lodges that had not paid their dues. Boardman was elected by 60 votes to 14 and the 'troublemakers' withdrew. In June 1808 the Grand East of Ulster was formed with (reputedly) the representatives of 311 lodges who met at Dungannon. This body was also sometimes styled the Grand East of Ireland and the Grand Lodge of Ulster.

[69] Ref: GBR 1991 HC 15/B/16 in the Library and Museum of Freemasonry, London.

On 3rd November 1808 a letter from the Grand Lodge of Scotland was read in the Grand Lodge of Ireland:

> The Grand Lodge of Ireland will at all times most heartily concur with the Grand Lodge of Scotland in every measure which may tend to the general good of the Craft and particularly in giving its most Zealous support to the maintenance of good order, subordination & respect for authority which must form the basis of every social compact & without which no Society either private of public can possibly exist

In December 1808 a further reassurance came from the Earl of Moira speaking for both the Moderns Grand Lodge in England and the Grand Lodge of Scotland

> I can answer for the cordial cooperation of the Grand Lodges of England & Scotland in maintaining the due authority (as far as their influence may operate) of the Grand Lodge of Ireland. For these bodies are deeply impress'd by the mischief which must arise to the Craft, as well as the danger to the State, if Masonic Lodges can be permitted to assume an independence of the Grand Lodge.[70]

The last references to the Grand East of Ulster come as mention of a public procession in 1813, and in the International Compact of 1814. The victory at Waterloo and the defeat of Napoleon were in the future, the country was fractious and the example of Masonic insurrection in Ireland was a warning to England. The evidence of the support of all the Grand Lodges of the United Kingdom for the Grand Lodge of Ireland against the Grand East of Ulster, and the words used, make a very clear statement about the need to keep order.

The traditional view has been that Boardman was the innocent party in these events. He certainly gave many years of devoted effort to Irish freemasonry but was clearly out of touch with views outside Dublin in the first decade of the nineteenth century. As a person one can more easily feel empathy with Boardman than with Seton. Seton, being in the right place at the right time, came to lead events.

When it came to the Earl of Moira and the Duke of Sussex deciding what was possible in an English Masonic Union, they might well have

---

[70] These quotes are from J H Lepper and P Crossle *History of the Grand Lodge of Ireland Vol.1* (1925) p382. The history contains a full account of the events of the 'Seton Secession' in Chapter 8 pp321-406.

decided to take due notice of events in Ireland and adopt a risk-minimising and prudential strategy.

Francis Rawdon Hastings, Earl of Moira (1754-1826)
Acting Grand Master Moderns 1795-1816
Acting Grand Master Scotland 1806-1808

Chapter 9 – Scotland, the Prince of Wales and the Earl of Moira

While Ireland was involved in all sorts of difficulties, the situation in Scotland was very different. It is worth going back a few years and first of all to England to understand developments. At the Quarterly Communication (of the Moderns) of 7th February 1787 it was stated that the Prince of Wales (HRH George Augustus Frederick (1762-1830)) had been initiated into Freemasonry at a special lodge held at the Star and Garter, Pall Mall on the previous evening. At the next Quarterly Communication it was agreed that he would be given the rank of Past Grand Master.

The Prince of Wales was elected Grand Master on 24th November 1790[71], and the Earl of Effingham appointed Acting Grand Master. Some

---

[71] RF Gould *History of Freemasonry Volume II* pages 483-484. Gould gives more details. It is worth remembering too that as a result of the illnesses of George III, that the Prince

seven years later in May 1795 the Earl of Moira, later the Marquis of Hastings was appointed Acting Grand Master in the place of Effingham, an office he kept until he departed for India in early 1813. Thus began one of the more remarkable, and least written about partnerships in British freemasonry, that of the Earl of Moira and several of the six sons of George III, five of whom became freemasons. This was an age in which freemasonry came as close to the centre of the social establishment of Britain as it was possible to be.

The Prince who did not become a mason was the Duke of Cambridge. Of the other Princes, Frederick, Duke of York, was initiated in Britannic Lodge No.28 on November 1787. Edward, Duke of Kent, in the Union Lodge in Geneva. Ernest, Duke of Cumberland, was made a mason at the house of the Earl of Moira in May 1796. Augustus, Duke of Sussex, was initiated in the Royal York Lodge of Friendship, Berlin in 1798. William, later the Duke of Gloucester, the nephew and son-in-law of the King was also initiated in Britannic Lodge in 1795. Their acquaintance with freemasonry did not end at the Craft[72] for the Duke of Gloucester got the degrees of the Swedish Rite when on a visit to Sweden while the Duke of Sussex obtained all the possible degrees while in Berlin. It is a long list but it is also a reflection upon the European-ness of the Royal Princes. However a decade later, and in the midst of the Napoleonic Wars, the Royal family might desire to be seen as being more positively British.

North of the Border in 1803 masonically strange events were about to take place, for at the meeting of the Grand Lodge of Scotland on 30th November 1803 the historian Laurie records that:

> The Brethren having re-assembled at the Kings Arms Tavern in the evening to celebrate the festival of St. Andrew, were honoured with the company of his Excellency the Earl of Moira, Commander-in-Chief of his Majesty's

---

of Wales was appointed Prince Regent and thus performed many of the duties of the monarch from 1811-1820. It was in 1812 that he decided that his Masonic duties on top of his state duties were simply too onerous and consequently he stepped aside, becoming Past Grand Master, and the Duke of Sussex took his place.

[72] The use of the word 'Craft', an allusion to the craft of stonemasonry, is a word used among freemasons to describe the first three degrees of freemasonry. These three degrees are under the authority of a Grand Lodge. There are many other degrees, separately administered by other bodies.

Forces in Scotland, and Acting Grand Master of the Grand Lodge of England[73].

Laurie goes on to recall the traditional recognition of the Antients Grand Lodge. He attributed it largely to the Duke of Atholl being Grand Master of the Antients. His next fascinating paragraph reads as follows:

> In the course of the evening, however, an opportunity being offered for the discussion of the subject, the Earl of Moira, in an eloquent and impressive address, related at considerable length the conduct of the Grand Lodge of England to the Ancient Masons, and stated that the hearts and arms of the Grand Lodge to which he was attached, had ever been open for the reception of their seceding Brethren, who have obstinately refused to acknowledge their fault; and that, through the Grand Lodge of England differed in a few trifling observations from that of Scotland, they had ever entertained for Scottish Masons that affection and regard which it is the object of Free Masonry to cherish, and the duty of Free Masons to feel.

A year later in 1804 the Grand Master Mason of Scotland stated that Scotland had long been anxious to open a fraternal intercourse with the Grand Lodge of England and Resolutions to that effect had been passed at a previous meeting "which he begged leave now to present to the Earl of Moira" – who was present. And, not surprisingly, on 5th August 1805 the Grand Lodge of England (under the Prince of Wales) responded. From that point events moved fast for on the 2nd December 1805 the Prince of Wales was elected Grand Master Mason, the Rt.Hon. George, Earl of Dalhousie Acting Grand Master and his Excellency Francis, Earl of Moira, Commander-in-Chief for Scotland, voted Acting Grand Master Elect. Thus a year later the Earl of Moira became Acting Grand Master of Scotland from 1806 to 1808 while the Prince of Wales remained Grand Master until he ascended to the throne in 1820. In all of this, and perhaps most importantly, there is no mention of any rupture of the relationship between Scotland and the Antients, of whom the Duke of Atholl was of course Grand Master, and with whom they had established a state of "constant correspondence" upon his succession in 1772. This recognition seems today curious because Scotland was recognising two competing

---

[73] W A Laurie, *The History of Freemasonry and the Grand Lodge of Scotland*, Edinburgh 1859. The events are recounted at length starting on p167. This book is out of copyright and obtainable online as a pdf file. St Andrews Day, 30th November, is in Scotland the traditional day on which the annual installation meetings of the Grand Lodge take place.

Grand Lodges, and clearly saw nothing wrong in doing that - an example of pragmatic good practice that might be revived today to some advantage! At the same time as these conciliatory moves between England and Scotland were happening mayhem was about to break out among Irish freemasonry.

Perhaps we need to know a little more about the Earl of Moira (1754-1826)[74]. He was born at the family home in Moira, Co. Down and grew up there and in Dublin, attended Harrow and afterwards Oxford University. He fought in the American War of Independence and in 1789 on the death of a maternal uncle received a substantial inheritance. He succeeded his father in 1793 becoming the 2nd Earl of Moira. He became an intimate friend of the Prince of Wales and an active freemason and so we see both of them appearing in English and Scottish freemasonry. In 1797 Moira published a speech on "the dreadful and alarming state of Ireland" and was a supporter of Catholic Emancipation. His (Whig) political inclinations thus perhaps shared some sympathy with those of the Prince of Wales. Events also indicate that as a person he was often of an inclination to try and seek common ground and unanimity among those of divergent views. In 1803, when he appeared in Edinburgh at the Grand Lodge of Scotland he had just been appointed as Commander-in-Chief of the Army there and promoted to General. He was politically active as well and had hopes of high office there which were never fulfilled. In 1812 he was appointed Governor General of British India, a position he held for some nine years before becoming ill and retiring to a kinder climate in Malta. He suffered greatly with his finances and was much in debt though it seems not so much through profligate personal expenditure but from his generosity to others.[75] Clearly not only was he a man of diplomacy and reason – as having held major posts in the Empire he was also a man of considerable organisational skills.

---

[74] Masonically the best work is that of John Hamill's 'The Earl of Moira, Acting Grand Master 1790-1813' in *AQC* Vol.93 pp31-48.

[75] The *Oxford Dictionary of National Biography* contains an excellent and balanced account of Moira's life. In particular it deals with his political life, his financial travails and his relationship with the Prince Regent. 1812 was a year in which his neither his political life nor relationship with the Prince Regent went well. At the end it was at the Prince's recommendation that he was offered the post in India.

In 1806 Moira spoke in Grand Lodge (Moderns) of his recent visit to the Grand Lodge of Scotland. His speech was couched in terms that suited the meeting but one short section is worth more careful consideration for it may well be that the use of language has changed and is today different from 200 years or more ago.

> That the Brethren of the Grand Lodge of Scotland were desirous that the strictest union and most intimate communications should subsist between this Grand Lodge and the Grand Lodge of Scotland and as a first step towards so important an object and in testimony of the wishes of the Scottish Freemasons, H.R.H. The Prince of Wales had been unanimously elected Grand Master of Scotland.[76]

John Hamill in his paper in AQC Vol.93 finds this speech of Moira's 'surprising for two reasons: first that it expressed a wish for a union with Scotland rather than just friendly relations'. However there had been previous exchanges for on 5th August 1805 a letter from the Grand Secretary of the Moderns in London to the Grand Lodge of Scotland was read which noted that Scotland 'had expressed through the Right Honorable the Earl of Moira its earnest wish to be on terms of confidential communication with the Grand Lodge of England under the authority of the Prince of Wales, this Grand Lodge, therefore, ever desirous to concur in a fraternal intercourse with regular Masons...and requests the honour of the Acting Grand Master to make such declaration in its name to the Grand Lodge of Scotland'.[77]

At this same meeting Scotland appointed a committee to '...thank the Earl of Moira for his attention in bringing about this desirable union'[78]. Thus it is clear that whatever union was expected had clearly been achieved and it was not a union of merger between the two Grand Lodges.

There seems to be some lack of clarity about what is meant by the word 'union' and consulting the Shorter Oxford English Dictionary – and two alternative meanings are offered. Firstly 'The act of uniting one thing to another so as to form a complete body' and secondly 'The uniting together of the different sections, parties or individuals of a nation or

---

[76] Minutes, premier Grand Lodge 1806.

[77] W A Laurie, *History of Free Masonry and the Grand Lodge of Scotland* pp169-170.

[78] W A Laurie, *History of Free Masonry and the Grand Lodge of Scotland* pp169-170.

other body so as to produce a general agreement or concord'. Thus given the fuller view of correspondence, and of a similar use of the words in the Antients' minutes[79], what Moira was referring to was not a union into one body, but that of producing a general concord. Clearly in the early 19th century the word was easily used in both contexts whereas today only the meaning of forming a single body would be current usage.

George Augustus Frederick Prince of Wales, later George IV
(1762-1830)
Grand Master Grand Lodge of England 1792-1812, Grand
Master Mason Scotland 1806-1820

---

[79] In *QCA* Vol.11, 'Early Records of the Grand Lodge of England according to the Old Institutions' p101. The Antients on 1st March 1758 in reading a letter from Ireland agreeing to 'keep a Constant Correspondence', and assuring 'the Grand Lodge of Antient Masons in London that the Grand Lodge in Ireland did mutually concur in a strict Union with the Antient Grand Lodge in London'. There is no doubt whatsoever that Ireland were not looking to create as the dictionary says 'a complete body' but simply 'a general agreement or concord'.

There are two Scottish events that also deserve a mention.

At the Quarterly Communication of 7th November 1807 the Lodge of Perth and Scoon was, upon a memorial to that effect, readmitted into the bosom of Grand Lodge, from which for some years past she had been estranged; and considering the great antiquity of this Lodge, and the handsome manner in which her office-bearers offered to pay up all arrears, the Grand Lodge re-instated her in her old number on the Roll of Daughter Lodges.[80]

The second is that on 14th October 1807 the committees of the Grand Lodge of Scotland and the Mother Lodge of Kilwinning met and drew up a Minute of Agreement which they all signed. While Mother Kilwinning renounced the right to grant charters she brought with her all Lodges holding under her, was placed at the head of the Roll of the Grand Lodge[81], and the Master of the Lodge would thenceforth be designated the Provincial Grand Master for the Ayrshire district. At the November Quarterly Communication of the Grand Lodge of Scotland the report of the committees was approved.

Thus in one year, 1807, Scotland had consolidated its position by bringing two old lodges into the fold of Grand Lodge. One might well suspect that the Earl of Moira, being Deputy Grand Master in 1805 and Acting Grand Master in 1806 and 1807, had a hand in all of this. What was not in doubt is that Scotland was not going to be preoccupied with dissident lodges for the next few years and that was borne out by the confident stance taken by Scotland in recognising both English Grand Lodges in 1810.

In Scotland on 25th October 1809, the day of the national celebrations commemorating the 50th year of the reign of George III, a foundation stone was laid for the George the III's Bastion at the Port of Leith, in a ceremony performed by the Right Honourable the Earl of Moira, in

---

[80] W A Laurie, *History of Freemasonry and the Grand Lodge of Scotland* 1859 p176. Laurie notes that at the time of writing the Lodge of Perth and Scoon had minute books going back some 300 years. Such matters are of course debated in Scotland, and in England, probably unjustifiably, viewed with at least strong scepticism.

[81] When the Grand Lodge of Scotland was formed in 1736 a roll of lodges had to be constructed. As one might imagine, getting this established to the satisfaction of all was a hard task. Kilwinning complained not only about precedence but also that the meeting was always to be in Edinburgh. The Lodge of Edinburgh was able to produce minutes going back to 1599 which was some 43 years older than anything that Kilwinning could produce. In 1743 after attempting, unsuccessfully, to get promoted to the head of the list of lodges, Kilwinning left the Grand Lodge and went its own way for some 70 years and resumed chartering lodges both in Scotland and in North America.

absence of the Most Worshipful the Acting Grand Master. In typical style he addressed those present and his words reflect interestingly upon both national and masonic situations.

> As Masons, we have further to boast a special obligation: When mischievous combinations on the Continent, borrowing and prostituting the respectable name of Masonry, had sown disaffection and sedition throughout the communities within which they were protected, and thereby called on the vigilance of the British Government to forbid particular confederacies, here a flattering discrimination exempted the established Freemasons from the scope of this prohibition. On the sole pledge of our declaration, - on the simple security of our good faith, there was manifested a generous trust in our Ancient Fraternity.[82]

These were difficult political times for Britain. The country had been at war almost continually with France since 1793 and there were bad harvests and food riots. Nelson won the Battle of Trafalgar in 1805 but the Battle of Waterloo was still some years away (1815). Maybe the Hanoverians felt they needed to demonstrate their Britishness, and freemasons to demonstrate their loyalty. And of course the Scots to demonstrate their loyalty to Britain, while of course retaining their essential Scottishness and gently declining English attempts at dominance. A unity of purpose needed to be demonstrated, and it duly was.

In London the Moderns minutes of 12th April 1809 record that they resolved to revert to the Ancient Landmarks while on 8th June 1810 the Antients agreed that the three Grand Lodges must all agree to work in the same forms. The moves towards Union were gathering some momentum.

At the meeting of the Grand Lodge of Ireland on 7th June 1810 they received a report from the committee appointed to consider the admission of Modern Masons into Irish Lodges. The committee begged to decline giving an opinion 'in view of the negotiations then on foot in England towards a Union'. Seemingly Ireland considered that the Moderns had reverted to the Ancient workings of their own accord and because of that the question of admission without remaking became a relevant question. Little could they know that it was to take another six years before there was an agreed (but perhaps in reality an imposed) ritual of the United Grand Lodge of England!

Ireland had received a letter from Bro Leslie, Grand Secretary of the Antients (as had Scotland), and after it had been read they resolved that:

---

[82] W A Laurie, *History of Freemasonry and the Grand Lodge of Scotland,* 1859 p179.

The Grand Lodge of Ireland have receiv'd with inexpressible satisfaction a communication from their Worshipful Bro Leslie Gr. Secy. of the Grand Lodge of England containing certain resolutions tending to a Masonic Union of the Grand Lodge (of Antients and Moderns)…..

That the Grand Lodge of Ireland are of the opinion that the resolution of the Grand Lodge of England agreed to on the first of May, 1810 ought to form the basis upon which the re-union of the two Grand Lodges shou'd be founded but herein the Grand Lodge of Ireland desire only to apply their opinion to general principles, submitting the minor arrangements to the adjustment of the Grand Officers of the respective Grand Lodges.

That the Grand Officers of the Grand Lodge of Ireland now in London, be requested and are hereby authoris'd to cooperate in the further progress and final settlement of this important work.

This reversion to the Ancient workings by the Moderns placed Ireland in an odd position in their masonic jurisprudence terms. By all Irish standards this reversion to Ancient working and thus to the ancient landmarks made such Modern brothers now regular masons and thus entitled to admission. However in 1812 when brethren of the Royal Westminster Militia (Lodge of Harmony No.583 EC) had sought admission into Lodge No.521 in Newry they were refused. The Militia brethren referred the matter to the Grand Lodge of Ireland and were, eventually, answered some 9 months later. Ireland were sorry for the difference of opinion but 'did not feel it possible to make any order for the admission of Modern Masons into Ancient Lodges until a final determination is made between the Grand Lodges of England under the Duke of Atholl & Prince Regal which they are informed is at present suspended'.

The response of the Grand Lodge of Scotland was entirely different in both tenor and decision for at an Extraordinary General Meeting of the Grand Lodge of Scotland held on 14th day of June 1810[83]:

---

[83] The Unanimous Resolution passed by the Grand Lodge of Scotland is of course recorded in the minute book of the Grand Lodge of Scotland and the letter sent to London can be seen at the Library and Museum of Freemasonry in London – Ref GBR12/A/7. Its contents are unusual and are quoted at length. Today it is the firm and oft stated practice for a Grand Lodge to recognise only one Grand Lodge in any territory but on this occasion we can see the Scots as a matter of expediency and practicality recognising two competing Grand Lodges. Pragmatism may have some advantages in achieving practical and diplomatic progress: it certainly did in 1810!

The Right Worshipful William Inglis Esquire Acting Substitute Grand Master under his Royal Highness The Prince of Wales Grand Master Mason and Patron of the Order in Scotland in the Chair.

The Grand Secretary submitted to the Meeting a letter received from the RW Brother Leslie Secretary to the Grand Lodge of Masons in England under the Duke of Athol enclosing a copy of the Resolutions of the Grand Lodge of England in consequence of a Negociation which has opened for accomplishing a Union between the Grand Lodge of England under His Royal Highness the Prince of Wales and the Grand Lodge of Masons under the Most Noble The Duke of Athol.

The above letter and Resolutions having been read and duly considered The Grand Lodge of Scotland Resolved Unanimously that it will at all times afford the Grand Lodge of Scotland the most sincere pleasure to cooperate with the Grand Lodges of England in every measure that may promote the general welfare of freemasonry. And they do therefore unanimously appoint the following Grand Officers or any one of them MW the Hon[ble] and Most Worshipful William Maule of Panmure MP Acting Grand Master of Scotland under his Royal Highness the Prince of Wales and the Right Hon[ble] and Right Worshipful the Earl of Moira Past Grand Master of Scotland with full and ample powers to them or any one of them to convene with the officers of the respective Grand Lodges of England to assist and concur in any measures that may be adopted by the Sister Grand Lodges for the permanent union and the general Interest Honour and Harmony of the Masonic Order.

…..Resolved unanimously that Copies of these Resolutions be transmitted to the Grand Lodges of England under His Royal Highness the Prince of Wales and His Grace the Duke of Athol and that copies be transmitted to the Hon William Maule the Earl of Roslyne and the Earl of Moira as the authority to them or any of them in name of the Grand Lodge of Scotland to the above effect.

The contrast between the Scottish and Irish positions is marked with the Scots clearly encouraging the two English Grand Lodges to reach an agreement while itself remaining aloof from involvement in the detail.

Seny sculp.

HRH Prince Edward Duke of Kent (1767-1820)
Provincial Grand Master (Antients) for Lower Canada 1791-1800
Grand Master (Antients) 1813

Chapter 10 - What was Antientness?
Or Alternatively: The Special Lodge of Promulgation (1809-1811) & Lodge of Reconciliation (1813-1816)[84]

Trying to discover just what Antientness was has proved to be a hard thing for many researchers. A couple of bland statements regarding the transposition of the words of the first and second degrees following the publication of Samuel Prichard's *Masonry Dissected* is somehow not enough. One would think that there has to be more than that, but attempts to disentangle reality from supposition seems to lead nowhere in particular. One would expect the best hints to lie in the proceedings of the Special Lodge of Promulgation and the Lodge of Reconciliation. But…

---

[84] The best bibliography for these events are the papers by:
W B Hextall, The Special Lodge of Promulgation: 1809-1811 in *AQC* Vol.23 (1910) pp37-71. W Wonnacott, The Lodge of Reconciliation: 1813-1816 in *AQC* Vol.23 (1910) pp 215-307. A more recent and accessible paper is by C J Mandleberg, 'Promulgation and Reconciliation', is in *AQC* Vol.123 pp77-123.

The Special Lodge of Promulgation was warranted, by the Moderns, on 26th October 1809 to continue until the 31st December 1810 and no longer (!). Its purpose was stated in the warrant to be 'for the purpose of Promulgating the Antient Landmarks of the Society and instructing the Craft in all such matters and forms as may be necessary to be known by them…'. However by the time of the circular sent to the elected members announcing the meeting of 21st November the wording had become 'for the purpose of ascertaining and promulgating the Ancient Landmarks of the Craft'. Perhaps a realization had dawned that it might be rather more difficult to work out what was Modern, what was Ancient and what had simply just become different over time and repetition. They seemed initially to meet every week and they did record in general terms the matters discussed, without of course disclosing anything that was 'not to be written'.

December 8th 1809. '…respecting the mode of placing the three Great Lights, seating of the Wardens, and opening the Lodge in the First Degree' were among the issues discussed. The ceremony of rehearsing the Ancient Charges before closing the lodge was recognised and resolved on (this of course raised the question about whether they were read after opening or before closing).

December 13th. They 'Resolved that Deacons (being proved on due investigation to be not only Ancient but useful and necessary Officers) be recommended'.

December 29th. They resolved that the situation of the Past Masters should be a the subject of future discussion. The Duke of Sussex was present.

January 23rd 1810. The Antient mode of Adjourning to refresh and returning to Labour were practiced (which of course implies that the Moderns did not do this). The Minutes noted that they enjoyed a good dinner with plenty of practice toasting.

February 16th. A resolution was passed affirming the mode of closing in the third degree, ending with ' but that Masters of Lodges shall be informed that such of them as may be inclined to prefer another known method of communicating the S[t] in the Closing ceremony will be at liberty to direct it if they should think proper to do so'.

April 27th. The master of the lodge made a reference to 'the near prospect of a union with the Atholl Lodges…'. And indeed he was right for Scotland soon after recognised both Antients and Moderns on 14th June 1810 and the text included the words 'a Negotiation which has opened for accomplishing a Union'.

The meeting on 11th May was the last before the summer break and the lodge reconvened on 19th October. A break of some 5 months!

19th October. 'Resolved that it appears to this Lodge that the ceremony of Installation of Masters of Lodges is one of the two Landmarks of the Craft and ought to be observed'. This sentence has prompted much opinion by researchers. Everything from the thought that two is an error to others wondering what the other one might actually be.

14th December. 'Resolved that a Memorial be presented to the Grand Master for renewal of the warrant for two months'. (which was granted).

5th March 1811. A further petition had been sent to the Grand Master for the renewal of the lodge for another year. The Grand Master declined saying that 'he conceived it would not be advisable to authorise the further continuance of the Labours of the Lodge…' and agreed only to a one month extension. At the end of March 1811 the minute book of the Lodge of Promulgation closes with tributes to all the members.

Almost a year earlier the Antients had set out various conditions to the Moderns and on 8th March 1811 got a reply, an assurance regarding the Ancient Landmarks, another on Obligations and a response the Antients found unsatisfactory regarding representation at Grand Lodge. It had been the custom among Antients' lodges to install masters on both St John's Days each year[85], but the Moderns lodges only once each year. If this practice continued then allowing all Antients Masters a place in Grand Lodge meetings would give them a big advantage in any vote. It seems that the high hopes of mid-1810 had vanished. Why?

---

[85] The two Saints John are the patron saints of freemasonry and their feast days are St John the Baptist on 24th June and St John the Evangelist on 27th December. Traditionally these were the days on which masters of lodges were installed and the Antients chose to do this twice a year, though they often put good masters back into the chair for another period or two. These days June is in the summer close season and the 27th December has become part of the extended Christmas. Therefore the practice no longer continues. Some lodges still celebrate what is known as the 'Festival of St John' on whatever date they install their masters.

While the Lodge of Promulgation had been busy, both at work and play it has to be said the Antients committee continued without any delegated powers to make decisions and even these most minor points had to be sent up to Grand Lodge for decision. Eventually it must have become obvious to the Earl of Moira, Acting Grand Master, that trying to arrange matters this way seemed increasingly unlikely to produce a result. Moira and Atholl tried to get the Antients Grand Lodge to agree with their view that the committee should have powers to negotiate. On 8th May 1811 the proposition was put. As the minutes record 'After some discussion and long debate thereon, and the question being put, passed in the negative by a large majority'. Moira had had enough and he instructed William White the Grand Secretary to write to the Antients and a draft of the letter in Moira's hand[86] includes the words:

> I am directed by his Lordship and the Committee to acquaint you for the information of the Grand Lodge under His Grace the Duke of Atholl that it appears to them wholly unnecessary and nugatory that any further meeting of the two Committees should take place at present, in as much as the committee of the Grand Lodge under the Duke of Atholl is not furnished with any sufficient powers to enter into the discussion or arrangement of the various subjects necessary to the proposed Union, as is sufficiently manifest from the circumstances of the Grand Lodge under his Grace the Duke of Atholl having at different times negatived propositions its Committee had acceded to, thereby annulling and frustrating the concessions which the Grand Lodge under His Royal Highness the Prince of Wales had professed itself, upon certain points, willing to make. I am further directed by His Lordship and the Committee to acquaint you that when ever the Committee from your Grand Lodge shall be invested with the powers specified in my letter of 26th January last, the Committee of the Grand Lodge under His Royal Highness the Prince Regent will be most ready to meet and confer with them...

A blunt letter and very much to the point. The Antients soon gave their committee the required powers. However the moment in 1810 for executing the Union had been lost. In December 1811 the Antients conceded to the Moderns practice of having but one Master per year (thus evening up the balance of power for voting in Grand Lodge).

---

[86] Library and Museum of Freemasonry, London. Historical correspondence GBR 1991 HC 12/A/39a-c.

The hiatus between the closure of the Lodge of Promulgation at the end of March 1810 and the start of any renewal of serious public effort towards a Union was to last until November 1813 – <u>a gap of over two years!</u>

Early in 1813 the Earl of Moira departed to take up his position in India and in May the Prince of Wales stood down and the Duke of Sussex became Grand Master. The Duke of Atholl retired as Grand Master of the Antients on 8th November and the Duke of Kent took his place. Interestingly the Duke of Sussex was made an Antient mason in a nearby room so he could be present at the Installation of his brother. The Articles of Union were signed on 25th November and afterwards ratified by both Grand Lodges on the same day, 1st December 1813.

On that day both Grand Lodges had agreed under Article V to appoint 'nine worthy and expert Master Masons', which they did. The members had largely already served in connection with the Union so the work of the Lodge of Promulgation was not wasted. Each Grand Lodge also created a Lodge of Reconciliation; to be later merged into one upon the Union being consummated. The Antients did this on the 1st December by issuing a dispensation, while the Moderns agreed on the same day but had to issue a warrant which was done on 7th December. It seems that being two lodges they took it in turns to occupy the offices and met that December on 10th, 14th, 16th, 17th, 20th, 21st and 22nd and then on St John's Day they retired to an adjoining room 'where those things that cannot be written' were found to be satisfactory. It might all have been a rush but on the second run there were not going to be any delays, even if matters of detail had to be sorted out after the event.

The reality of finding a form of ritual that was acceptable was to take longer than one might hope but probably no longer than it would take today's masons to attempt the same thing. Indeed progress was sufficiently slow that instructions were issued to the Craft at large that it was 'deemed desirable to issue instructions to all lodges that they were to "carry on" as they had hitherto been accustomed, pending further notice'. A letter was also sent in February 1814 to each lodge informing them that they were to accept the Obligations of each Fraternity and to cordially mix together. At the bottom was this:

In consequence of the Lodges holding under the two former Grand Lodges being now intermingled and incorporated in one list, the new Number of your Lodge on such United List is No.___ instead of No.___.

By command of the Most Worshipful the Grand Master[87]

The Lodge of Reconciliation did not meet between February and August 1814 and the March Quarterly Communication tells us why. 'It having been thought advisable to postpone the Meetings of the Lodge of Reconciliation until after the arrival of the Brethren from Scotland and Ireland…'. While it is not mentioned we might well expect that the members of the Lodge of Reconciliation demonstrated the adopted ritual of the new United Grand Lodge, a similar style of performance to the one they had delivered on the day of the Union.

There were of course some objections to the new rituals, in particular from nine London lodges, in relation to 'the forms of the Obligations to be given in the several degrees'. All the complaining lodges were Antients' lodges! In November 1814 they decided upon a 'memorial' which was sent to the Grand Master, who promptly passed it over to the Lodge of Reconciliation.

The Memorialists, as they were called, were heard by the Lodge of Reconciliation[88]. It seems that the biggest issue was the Obligations, especially in the first degree. The Lodge drafted a report for the Duke of Sussex in which they included the following:

> …the principal objections seemed to be against the 1st Obl^n. as delivered by the Lodge of Reconciliation, to which objections the Lodge replied by such arguments as proved it was more strong and effectual than any obl^n. before in use.

The matter had of course to be dealt with and on 23rd August 1815, at an open meeting, with the Duke of Sussex presiding:

> The Ancient Obl^gn of the 1st and 2nd degrees were then repeated, the former from the Throne, when it was RESOLVED and ORDERED that the same be recognised and taken in all time to come, as the only pure and genuine

---

[87] W Wonnacott, *The Lodge of Reconciliation: 1813-1816* in *AQC* Vol.23 (1910) p228.

[88] Wonnacott in *AQC* Vol.23 on page 239 quotes some comments from the minutes of the Lodge. One Memorialist saying 'I object to it because it is not so strong as the one I took…' and another who when asked what he objected to said 'To the whole, because the language is altogether altered and the differences are of great magnitude'.

Obs. of these Degrees, and which all Lodges dependent on the Grand Lodge shall practice

And

Forms and Ceremonies were then exhibited by the Lodge of Reconciliation for the Opening and Closing of Lodges in the three Degrees, which were also ordered to be used and practiced.

On the 4th September 1816 the Lodge of Reconciliation met for the last time and their minutes record that 'the W. Master, Officers and Brethren were awarded the thanks of the Grand Lodge for their unremitting Zeal and Exertion in the cause of Freemasonry.'

There seems little doubt that the Moderns conceded on all points of ritual where there ceremonies differed from those of the Antients. And of course they did not only have to satisfy the Antients but also the Scots and Irish who also practised something that was accepted as being 'Ancient'. This was an essential part of achieving internal masonic peace and harmony while the outside world was filled with strife and unrest.

Henry Sadler in his *Masonic Facts and Fictions*[89] sums up the problems when he says 'the great difficulty I, in common with everyone else who has written on this subject, have to encounter, is in ascertaining the differences that existed in the recognised forms of the two rival societies'.

When Samuel Prichard published his *Masonry Dissected*[90] and it ran to many editions it became, not the first, but the most public exposure of masonic ritual. How accurate it was is perhaps not important but because of its sheer popularity it became the *de facto* standard, and that well before

---

[89] Henry Sadler, *Masonic Facts and Fictions: Comprising a New Theory of the Origin of the Antient Grand Lodge*. It was first published in 1887 and then reprinted in 1985 with an Introduction by John Hamill. A couple of sentences are worth quoting here for they say all that needs to be said about Henry Sadler. 'As a Masonic historian Sadler was meticulous in his attention to detail and scrupulous in his attention to factual truth.' 'Sadler was breaking new ground not just with his theory but by discussing the Antients at all. Snobbishly and derisorily dismissed by the Premier Grand Lodge as tradesmen and menials of little interest to anyone, the Antients continued to be ignored down to our times by all but Sadler'. The book can currently be previewed online or copies of the paperback reprint are available second hand.

[90] *Masonry Dissected* was published on 2nd October 1730, the second edition advertised on the 3rd October and published on the 21st October, the third advertised on the 23rd October and published on the 31st October. There were at least thirty editions in England and eight in Scotland and more elsewhere.

the Antients were formed. Because this exposure opened up the possibility of non-masons gaining entry to lodges, and either discovering the secrets or obtaining money from the charity fund, Grand Lodge had changed round the signs and words of the first and second degrees.

What we do know is that at the (Moderns) Grand Lodge on 12th April 1809 they noted that is was 'necessary no longer to continue in force those measures which were resorted to in, or about, 1739, respecting irregular masons and do therefore enjoin the several lodges to revert to the ancient Landmarks of the order'. This is interesting because while acknowledging that there were changes, the exact date of the changes was unclear. The difficulties experienced in returning to the original workings (that is pre Prichard and pre 1730), the Ancient workings (what common (?) ritual used say in Ireland and Scotland around 1810), show that the scale and difficulty of discovery, and then reaching agreement, and the magnitude of such a task had been grossly underestimated by those in charge who were setting the pace towards the Union. The English mason was probably as wedded to his ritual then as masons are today; one can envisage the problems!

Of course the changes were not only to do with ritual. For example Gould notes that the practice of the United Grand Lodge of England with regard to the selection of Grand Officers was (and is) that all the officers (with the sole exceptions of the Grand Master and Treasurer, who are the only elected officers) are appointed by the Grand Master. By comparison the 'Atholl' custom of electing all the Grand Officers, was in closer harmony with the 'Ancient Landmarks' as disclosed to us by the 'General Regulations' of 1723 – that is to say Anderson's Constitutions of the original 1717 Grand Lodge. Also in the Moderns Grand Lodge Past Masters were not considered as members of Grand Lodge, whereas in the Antients they were. The Antients practice was adopted (although there were concerns about the numbers who might come to meetings!) while the Antients conceded that lodges would only have one Master each year. Also the Moderns practice that only those who had served as Grand Stewards could become Grand Officers was allowed to lapse.

Antientness is clearly a matter of pride for those lodges whose origins were Antient and is manifested today in the form of The Association of

Atholl Lodges[91] whose website is at www.theantients.co.uk. Likewise there are those whose preferences draw them to The Premier Grand Lodge. Clearly both groups can find things that they value in being 'United' after two centuries.

The Duke of Kent

The role of the Duke of Kent in events leading up to the Union in 1813 may have been understated because when he is referred to he appears only a month before taking the place of the Duke of Atholl as Grand Master of the Antients. A typical view when asked what the role of the Duke of Kent was in the Union would be 'Not a lot'[92], Indeed that would have been my view had I not chanced upon a volume of *The Freemason* for 1892, and discovered an article on the Duke of Kent[93].

The Duke began his military training in 1785 in Germany and afterwards spent 1788-89 in Geneva, where he became a mason. The response of the Moderns to this was to make him Past Grand Master and to appoint him as Provincial Grand Master of Andalusia, effectively Gibraltar. In 1789 he was appointed colonel of the 7th Regiment of Foot but was returned home and posted to Gibraltar. He was ordered to Canada, apparently until his debts were paid off and Kent spent the first three years in Quebec. This was followed by seven years in Halifax, Nova Scotia, before he was finally allowed to return home after a fall from his horse in 1800. While his military career was perhaps not glorious his other

---

[91] The objectives of the Association are: The Association of Atholl Lodges exists to provide a focus for the common interests of those surviving Lodges which were warranted by the Grand Lodge of England according to the Old Institutions (the Atholl Grand Lodge 1751-1813). Its aim is to preserve the Atholl heritage by fostering and promoting fraternal links between all Atholl Lodges across the UK and around the world, and with other interested parties.

[92] Indeed that was precisely the view taken by John Mandleberg in his paper in AQC when he wrote that he has no evidence for the 'Not a Lot' view but describes his position as 'A think, not a know!'

[93] *The Freemason* Vol.28 (1892) in the Christmas Issue of Wednesday 21st December pp 1-2. This contains a long and interesting article on the masonic sons of George III and the role they played in the Union. This article refers back to *The Freemasons Magazine* Vol.4 pp13-14 (1795). Both the address and response are printed with an engraving of Prince Edward. There is no comment upon either the address or the response in either this or the next issue of the magazine.

interests are worth noting. He followed the social experiments of Robert Owen, voted for catholic emancipation and supported anti-slavery societies.

The article in *The Freemason* deals with his masonic activities in Canada. It seems that on his arrival he introduced himself as an Ancient mason and a letter of 27th December 1791 to the Grand Secretary of the Antients in London states that:

> His Royal Highness Prince Edward who has made himself known to our Brother Alexander Wilson (who was Substitute Grand Master for the Province of Lower Canada) as an Ancient Mason, and has consented under his signature to become Provincial Grand Master of Upper and Lower Canada...

> ...supplicate the Grand Lodge to send by the earliest ship a Warrant of constituting His Royal Highness Provincial Grand Master of Upper and Lower Canada.

At the March 1792 meeting of the Grand Lodge in London a warrant was conformed, but only for Lower Canada, a new Provincial Grand Master for Upper Canada being present and installed at that same meeting. With the Duke of Kent supporting the cause of Ancient masonry it prospered greatly, while the fortunes of the Moderns in Lower Canada did not do well at all. However on leaving Quebec for Nova Scotia an address was delivered to him in person, dated 8th January 1794, signed by both William Grand Deputy Grand Master of Modern Masons and Thomas Ainslie Deputy Grand Master of Ancient Masons which included the following sentence 'We have a confidential hope that, under the conciliating influence of your Royal Highness, the Fraternity in general of Freemasons in his Majesty's dominions will soon be united'. The Duke in his response of the same day writes 'You may trust that my utmost efforts shall be exerted, that the much wished for union of the whole Fraternity of Masons may be effected' and adds afterwards 'I sincerely hope to hear that at all times the utmost harmony reigns in your Masonic operations. (signed) Edward'.

A Special Communication of the Antients Grand Lodge was summoned for 18th May 1813. The brethren received His Royal Highness. The account included these words:

His Royal Highness further said that upon every occasion he should be happy to co-operate with them in exerting themselves for the preservation of the Rights and Principles of the Craft, and that, however desirable an Union might be with the other Fraternity of Masons, it should only be desirable if accomplished on the basis of the Ancient Institutions, and with the maintenance of all the rights of the Ancient Craft.

Bro. Harper the Antients Grand Secretary informed the Duke of Atholl, Grand Master, of a letter of 12th July from William White the Grand Secretary of the Moderns in which the Duke of Sussex requests a meeting with the Duke. Harper went on to suggest that

'…it would be extremely desirable if your Grace could be at this interview', and should that not be practicable then, 'in the event of your Grace not being able to be present, that you would be pleased to signify your pleasure as to our Royal Brother , the Duke of Kent being appointed to act instead on this occasion, His Royal Highness being firmly attached to the Ancient Craft and not disposed to concede any of its Rights, Privileges, or Ancient Landmarks'.

The reply of the Duke of Atholl dated Dunkeld July 30th 1813 was that it was going to be impossible for him to attend and that he was happy for the Duke of Kent to attend in his place.

Perhaps after all the Duke of Kent was more than just a supernumerary to the event and act of the Union. After all his 'Antientness' in Canada was volunteered not requested, as was the aspiration to an eventual Union among the Canadian brethren, and his positive response to that aspiration. In 1813 he had also satisfied both the Grand Secretary and Grand Master of the Antients of his genuine caring for its values does demonstrate more than a token interest. For me that is rather more involvement than 'Not a Lot'!

Count Jacob de la Gardie (1768-1842)
Swedish diplomat and Master of the First Lodge of the North, Sweden

Chapter 11 - St John's Day December 1813

Both the Antients and Moderns really wanted their Union to be blessed by Ireland and Scotland. But Ireland had severe reservations and gave a very firm diplomatic refusal. Scotland chose not to make the effort. In the absence of these two parties, with whom both Antients and Moderns shared territory in the British Empire, they had to see what they could do to make the best of a bad job. Of the visitors on St John's Day 1813, the day of enacting the Union, only two are named: the Most Worshipful His Excellency Count de Lagardie and the Most Worshipful Brother Dr Von Hess of the Grand Lodge of Hamburgh[94].

---

[94] WJ Hughan, *Memorials of the Union of 1813*, (Revised Edition 1913) p39. Brother Jonas Lewis von Hess M.D. does not feature again in events but it is worth recording a few details. He died in 1823 after a long illness. He had entered military life young but was apparently of a delicate physical constitution and thus left the army for the University of Konigsberg. He became a friend of the philosopher Emmanuel Kant. He wrote and travelled extensively and wrote an elaborate history of the City of Hamburgh. When patriots were required for the defence of the State of Hamburgh from attack by Napoleon, the gallant Dr Van Hess was appointed Generalissimo of these brave men (source his obituary in *The Gentleman's Magazine* Vol.XCIII Jan-June 1823 pp472-473). Of his Masonic career the author has nothing to hand. Although the first lodge in Hamburgh was recorded in 1737, England appointed a Provincial Grand Master in 1786.

Count Jacob Gustaf Pontusson de Lagardie was born in 1768 in a Swedish military family and was destined for a military career. He was Lt. Captain by the age of 24 but soon after moved into the civil service. His close relationship with the Royal Court must have helped him obtain an ambassadorial post in Vienna between 1799 and 1802. Masonically he had obtained all 11 degrees by 1811. The king, Carl XIII, was Master of the First Lodge of the North from 1808 till 1818 and Lagardie was his Depute Master. As a result of an indiscretion of a political nature he was appointed ambassador in Cadiz in May 1813. Due, so it seems, to long and repeated delays in finding a ship for Cadiz he ended up only leaving Sweden for England in mid November, finally arriving in London on 28th November. His arrival in England at this particular time has to therefore be a matter of coincidence, and not something planned.

Lagardie was present at the meeting of the Antients GL on the 1st December 1813, perhaps almost accidentally, and was also present at the Union meeting on the 27th December 1813. It is fascinating that he kept a diary of events and there are exchanges of letters as well. From the archives in Sweden the Swedish researcher the late Bro Bo Akerren has compiled the tale of events[95]. There are certain differences between the official accounts and those of Lagardie. These are recounted and make fascinating reading, because English freemasonry could very easily have taken a completely different direction to the one planned! The official minutes are:-

> The members of the Lodge of Reconciliation accompanied by the Most Worshipful His Excellency Count de Lagardje, the Most Worshipful Brother Dr Von Hess, of the Grand Lodge of Hamburgh, and other distinguished visitors, withdrew to an adjoining apartment, where, being congregated and tiled, the result of all the previous conferences was made known. …

> His Royal Highness was placed on the Throne by the Duke of Kent and the Count Lagardje, and solemnly obligated.

This Province prospered for many years until the 'success of French arms' when there could be no links with England. Because of this on February 11th 1811 the Grand Lodge of Hamburgh declared itself independent.

[95] Bo Y Akerren, 'London in December 1813: The Place and Time of a Momentous Encounter of English with Swedish Rites', *AQC* Vol.115 (2002) pp184-204. The author being Swedish had a great linguistic advantage and he built greatly upon the two short pieces by John Heron Lepper in *AQC* Vol.61 of 1946.

In his diary Lagardie left a record of the day's events[96]:

Already at 11 o'clock Mr Blacker appeared who had been sent by the Duke of Sussex to escort me to the Lodge. There a great number of ceremonies were seen; more than 800 persons were assembled. After the Acts had been read and the Committee of Union had withdrawn to an adjoining room, the two Dukes inquired if I would accompany them and allow the Committee to read the two proposals so that I might afterwards say whichever I found the most *right* one which they would then adopt. I thereupon went out and the Obligations according to the Old and to the New Systems were read to me with many Ceremonies. Without hesitation I preferred the Old one as being much the better and also most corresponding to our Swedish system.

On my return to the Grand Assembly I made this protestation aloud to the whole Lodge, and both Dukes then according to the Old Ritual placed the Bible in my hands and each kissed it. The Duke of Sussex having, as set out in the printed Ceremonial, been elected Grand Master, I sat down on the Throne he had used whereupon he kneeling received his Decorations pertaining to his new office out of my hands.

Lagardie also notes that "at 6.30 o'clock we departed to dinner which lasted until 1.30 o'clock in the morning". As he says "I went home at nearly 2 o'clock being I must confess rather tired of the 14 hours I had spent." And "This probably is the only instance where a Swede in London has been placed in such a position that, in an assembly of over 800 persons all standing, he alone is seated, also one of the Princes Royal kneeling before him. Knowing the noble pride of the English, it is of double worth to find oneself in such a casus as that wherein I found myself, and most likely neither I nor anybody else will ever again be."

---

[96] J H Lepper, 'Further Extracts from Diary of Count Jacob de la Gardie', *AQC* Vol.56 pp308-9

It is perhaps unusual to have such a personal account of events otherwise of a very grand and formal nature, but Lagardie's notes do offer a complementary view of the day. It was a day that changed freemasonry; the United Grand Lodge of England was created and became a force across the masonic world. The Union reinforced the idea that there should be only one Grand Lodge in every territory; something already achieved in Scotland and soon to occur in Ireland.

Earlier in his stay Lagardie had been at a meeting of the Antients GL whom he described as being the NEW system – meaning the Antients. However it was probably sufficient on the day to pronounce the new version acceptable - but quite what Lagardie preferred we will never actually know.

The Swedish system in England?

This Union would rid us from the large number of false brethren who are overrunning Europe, and of which at least 2/3 come from here (England).[97]
Count Lagardie writing to his Grand Master King Carl XIII on 21ˢᵗ December 1813

When Lagardie came to England it would seem that there was no thought of his masonic activity in England having any significance. Probably much the same could be said of the Duke of Sussex who until the written apologies for non-attendance by Ireland and Scotland would have had no idea that he might need anyone else to take on the role of blessing the Union. His letter of 13ᵗʰ December to Lagardie contains the following:

---

[97] In Sweden becoming a freemason was not easy, but knowledge of freemasonry had spread and Swedes who travelled elsewhere often became masons. Typically it was seamen, master mariners and captains, whose ships visited port towns in Scotland and England, especially on the East coast, who became masons. They could join very quickly and get their certificate in the time it took to offload one cargo and find and load another. One can just imagine the knock on the door of a lodge room in Sweden and the tyler to find outside a master mariner just home having brought back a shipload of salted herring across the North Sea – not amused. While this was good business for lodges in port towns (who took the degree fees and a year's subscription) it did little for Grand Lodges (who only usually ever got one fee at the beginning but no annual dues thereafter!). The mariner masons had pretty much become extinct during the nineteenth century.

In our conversations you convinced me that the idea I had created on the subject is the very base of the Grand Purpose. I instantly wish to pronounce my inclination totally to reform everything in those mysteries which is not immaculate and which are not very well known in this country and cannot be introduced without proper guidance. I do not have to tell you, my dear Count, that we will need to be very prudent in this undertaking because of the number of individuals with which I will have to deal, and the infinity of extravagant opinions amongst them'.

He adds that:

In Germany I have received all the blue and Scottish degrees which, to a certainty, exist (Perfected in the Royal Arch), Knight of St Andrew, Knight of the Sepulchre (which is related to the Templars (mas) of this Country).

And:

I shall be most pleased to devote myself to introduce this very system, but time will be needed as so will prudence, as I have pointed out in the beginning of this letter, as one must advance stepwise and without wronging the individuals, that is the landscape I have created for my moral and political life, and I believe in my public life to have demonstrated my precise keeping of promises.

After the meeting of the Union there were other exchanges of letters between the Count and Carl XIII, Grand Master of Sweden. Lagardie was getting frustrated at the total lack of progress on the part of the Duke of Sussex in England, and also by his Grand Master Carl XIII's insistence that the English adopt the first three degrees Swedish style and that <u>only</u> after that would the St Andrew's degrees be passed over and likewise after that the Chapter degrees.

There are several ways of interpreting these events. Certainly there is no hint at all that Lagardie came with a plan to convert England to the Swedish system of freemasonry but perhaps he saw an opportunity to influence change in England for the better and bring order. For as he said in his letter to Carl XIII of 3rd May

'...but so many difficulties arise that I, for my own part, can see no possibility to secure a union; with the Duke's zeal for the cause, with his inclination to find and receive information, the matter would be an easy one if it depended upon him alone to decide, and, what is still worse, is that the uttermost disorder and anarchy in the Lodges themselves undo every modification or rather every attempt to create orderliness, and is equally incompatible with the self indulgence and the national pride of the English

to in any way bring their rituals, which at times are most diverse, into line one with the other.'

Perhaps towards the end of his stay Count Lagardie was getting the measure of English freemasonry for when he uses the words disorder and anarchy he was not far wrong. Attempts of the Grand Lodge of Ireland in 1806 to introduce control over the Royal Arch, by making it part of the Grand Lodge of Ireland, totally failed and led ultimately to the Seton Rebellion and The Grand East of Ulster. The multiplicity of degrees worked by (some) lodges in England meant that apart from the Craft (or blue) degrees there was little if any control over what went on – very unlike the situation in Sweden.

For those unfamiliar with the structure of Swedish freemasonry some explanation may be useful at this point. The first lodge was founded in Stockholm in 1735, and it was titled The First Lodge of the North - the same lodge of which Lagardie was Depute Master. All Craft Lodges in Sweden work only the first three, or blue, degrees of Entered Apprentice, Fellowcraft and Master Mason, and are called St John's Lodges.

The second order of St Andrew's Lodges, the first lodge being established in 1756, works the fourth, fifth and sixth degrees. These are those of Apprentice and Companion of St Andrew as the 4th and 5th degrees and Master of St Andrew as the 6th and third degree in the series.

The third order, most commonly called Chapter, confer four degrees which are Very Illustrious Brother, Knight of the East (7th); Most Illustrious Brother, Knight of the West (8th); Enlightened Brother of St John's Lodge (9th) and Very Enlightened Brother of St Andrews Lodge (10th).

There are other differences between Swedish and Anglo-Saxon Freemasonry of today. The major two are that it only admits Christians as members (although brethren from elsewhere not professing Christianity may visit) and that the Grand Lodge of Sweden has control of the whole ten degrees of their freemasonry compared with Grand Lodges elsewhere who are only ever responsible for the first three degrees.

Intervisitation protocols for those degrees after the first three also shed some useful light. An English Royal Arch Mason may visit the St Andrew's Lodges while a Swede must have the 6th degree to be able to visit an English Royal Arch Chapter. When it comes to the Chapter degrees the situation is rather more obscure but there are some philosophical links between the 8th and 9th degrees in the Swedish Rite and the Great Priory (Knights Templar and Knights of Malta). The 8th Swedish degree is seen as being comparable with the 18th degree of the Rose Croix, the 10th degree with the 30th of the Rose Croix and the 11th with the 33rd degree.

Perhaps in passing one might reflect that Antients lodges typically worked the Royal Arch and Knights Templar degrees using only their Craft warrant and thus covered in some way or other all the Swedish degrees from the first up to somewhere around the eight or ninth. What Lagardie and King Carl XIII sought might have been achievable with the Antients as it fitted in fairly well with their style but the Duke of Sussex knew only too well that the Union alone was at least as much change as English freemasons would accept without trouble. This was a matter he had touched upon in his letter of 13th December 1813 to Lagardie already quoted.

So, and after many delays, the Union of the Antients and Moderns had taken place in a day that lasted more than twelve hours and no doubt in both grand and ample form and with a late return home for the participants. But in the aftermath much remained to be dealt with. At home the formal signing had to be put into practice, dislikes smoothed over, rituals to be brought into approximate likeness, a Supreme Grand Chapter formed - much to make or break the Union. Slightly further afield the essential reconciliation with Scotland and Ireland over the genuine Antientness of the new agreed English ritual had yet to take place. All this was complicated by the essentials of Scottish and Irish national and masonic identities which were not going to be subservient to those of a United Grand Lodge in England. Empire would complicate matters as well and was not at all well dealt with as we shall see. The Irish and Irish masons had always been viewed, especially in England and by English Lodges as rather more common, rather more raucous than their own English cultural and social styles. This indeed was possibly, even probably, the cause of the non-assimilation of Irish populated independent lodges in England into English masonry. The Irish Grand Lodge were keen to ensure that they, their military lodges, and their own excruciatingly painful national masonic issues were understood in

England at what was the best opportunity to air issues for many a decade and their own causes supported.

Memorial Plaque to Bro John Boardman in St Patricks
(Protestant) Cathedral, Dublin

Chapter 12 - The International Compact of 1814

INTERNATIONAL COMPACT
BETWEEN THE GRAND LODGES OF
ENGLAND, IRELAND, AND SCOTLAND.
CONCLUDED JULY 1814.

At a Conference held in FREE MASONS HALL, LONDON, on Monday, the 27th June, and continued by adjournment to Saturday the 2nd July, 1814, And of Masonry 5814.

The International Compact of 1814 is one of the strangest masonic documents in existence. The actual conference did take place but after the signing there was only silence and it was not until a century had passed that it was made public. The Irish masonic researcher W J Chetwode Crawley published the first version in 1914[98] and it was taken from the

---

[98] W J Chetwode Crawley, 'The International Compact', 1814 in *AQC* Vol.28 pp141-155.

Minutes of the Grand Lodge of Ireland meeting held on 1st December 1814. No other copy of the final signed document has been found in the archives of the records of the Grand Lodges of England and Scotland to this day.

This poses some interesting questions. Who felt that such an agreement was essential? Why was it needed? Why the silence in the records afterwards? Part of the explanation for the clauses themselves can be elucidated, but as to why it was never promulgated afterwards there is no evidence to help shed any light.

The invitation was sent from London and we have the reply of the Irish Deputy Grand Secretary from Dublin of 7th April 1814.[99]

> That the following Noblemen and Gentlemen Brothers be appointed Delegates to represent this Grand Lodge at the Grand Communication in London
>
> His Grace the Duke of Leinster, Grand Master
>
> Rt Honble Earl of Donoughmore M.W. P. Grand Master
>
> Honble Abm H-Hutchinson R.W.D. Grand Master
>
> R W John Boardman Esq Grand Treasurer
>
> Rt Honble Lord Henry Seyr Moore Master Lodge 857
>
> (Signed) By Order WF Graham DGS

We do know that Boardman attended the meeting of the United Grand Lodge of England in London on 9th May and from the plaque we know that he died in London on 29th May 1814 while 'on a mission to the United Grand Lodge of England'. Surely a rare memorial to a brother; and while the name of Boardman is not necessarily one viewed favourably by all Irish brethren he served the Grand Lodge of Ireland faithfully to the last. His early presence in London 'on a mission' some two months before the convened meeting shows just how seriously the pre-negotiations were being taken.

The Antients had, over three years earlier, at a Grand Lodge of Emergency held on 1st May 1810, set out its position. There were three points and the first dealt with the Obligations and Uniform Rules that they, the Antients, stated that they shared with Ireland and Scotland:

---

[99] Letter from Graham to the Grand Secretary of UGLE in London dated 7th April 1814. Ref HS/15/A/20 in the Library and Museum of Freemasonry in London.

I. That the Grand Lodges of the United Kingdom, Viz the Grand Lodge of England under the Most Noble the Duke of Atholl the Grand Lodge of Scotland and the Grand Lodge of Ireland are all bound by the same Obligations and all work by Uniform Rules it is necessary in the first instance to be informed whether the Grand Lodge under H.R.Highness the Prince of Wales in Order to make a perfect Union will consent to take the Same Obligations under which the three Grand Lodges [are bound] and that they will consent to work in the same forms.

Clause IV of the Articles of Union, signed on 1ˢᵗ December 1813, went on to set out the expectations for the approval of a common agreed form of ritual not only by the new United Grand Lodge of England but possibly also by the Grand Lodges of Scotland and Ireland. They largely reiterate the Antients' resolution of May 1810:

IV. To prevent all controversy or dispute as to the genuine and pure obligations, forms, rules and ancient traditions of Masonry, and further to unite and bind the whole Fraternity of Masons in one indissoluble bond, it is agreed that the obligations and forms that have, from, time immemorial, been established, used, and practised, in the Craft, shall be recognized, accepted, and taken, by the members of both Fraternities, as the pure and genuine obligations and forms by which the incorporated Grand Lodge of England, and its dependant Lodges in every part of the World, shall be bound : and for the purpose of receiving and communicating due light and settling this uniformity of regulation and instruction (and particularly in matters which can neither be expressed nor described in writing), it is further agreed that brotherly application be made to the Grand Lodges of Scotland and Ireland, to authorize, delegate and appoint, any two or more of their enlightened members to be present at the Grand Assembly on the solemn occasion of uniting the said Fraternities ; and that the respective Grand Masters, Grand Officers, Masters, Past Masters, Wardens and Brothers, then and there present, shall solemnly engage to abide by the true forms and obligations (particularly in matters which can neither be described nor written), in the presence of the said Members of the Grand Lodges of Scotland and Ireland, that it may be declared, recognized, and known, that they all are bound by the same solemn pledge, and work under the same law.

The absence of any representatives from either of the Grand Lodges of Ireland or Scotland on the 27ᵗʰ December 1813 must have been greatly felt by those planning the Union for they had an order of procession prepared which included the Grand Masters of Ireland and Scotland and their Wardens.[100] There can be no doubt that the Modern element having laboured hard to once again adopt the right degree of 'Antientness', which they had abandoned around 1739, must have felt that they needed the final endorsement of Ireland and Scotland to ensure a restoration of harmony. Maybe the Antients remained insistent upon this clause as well? But maybe Ireland and Scotland were somewhat anxious about exactly what 'working by Uniform Rules' and 'that the three Grand Lodges will consent to work in the same forms', might entail.

The final part of the clause is equivocal in what it expected from Ireland and Scotland and whether or not they to were going to be expected to 'bound by the same solemn pledge' or not. Neither was it clear what form of words was going to be used to ask Ireland and Scotland's approval. Ask a lawyer to offer an opinion on the wording of Article IV and they would advise caution to their client, and alternative implications would be subject to a lively debate between lawyers regarding possible interpretations. In the event Lagardie was asked to state his approval of a set of words he had heard and to do so publicly in front of all present; he at least had the advantage of being able to go home to Sweden without having made any commitment which might bind his Grand Lodge. Scotland and Ireland might not be so fortunate.

THE INTERNATIONAL COMPACT

It is worth examining the content of the clauses of the International Compact[101] one by one.

Clause 1 declared and pronounced that pure Ancient Masonry consisted of three Degrees, and no more ... including the Supreme Chapter of the Holy Royal Arch, and 'the latter part relative to the Supreme Grand Chapter'...'the undersigned promise to state to their respective Grand Lodges' and to communicate the result of this to the Duke of Sussex.

---

[100] W J Hughan in *Memorials of the Masonic Union of 1813* (1873) list the Order of Proceedings for the 27th December Union meeting. There were adopted at a meeting at Kensington Palace on 9th December 1813 p28.

[101] A copy of the full text of the International Compact was viewed in 2012 on the *Pietre-Stones Review of Freemasonry* website at http://www.freemasons-freemasonry.com/compact.html

The equivalent clause in the (earlier) Articles of Union of the 1st December instead referred to 'The Supreme Order of the Holy Royal Arch' and contained a sentence regarding the Orders of Chivalry. The Orders of Chivalry sentence had simply vanished in the period between December 1813 and June 1814!

In moving from Supreme Order to Supreme Chapter one can almost detect the hand of lawyers well versed in finding a wording upon which all could agree. If masonry required a Supreme Chapter then Ireland and Scotland could both agree that, because while they did not have one, they could agree that having one would be a good thing – whenever it might be something that happened in their country. Neither could Ireland nor would Scotland countenance a Supreme Order within their Grand Lodge and the agreed wording had to be such that it could not be construed to imply that. In the meantime England got what it probably needed to maintain peace between Antients and Moderns – Pure Ancient Masonry[102]!

Clause 2 states that 'constant fraternal intercourse, correspondence, and communion be for ever maintained'. This of course was something that Ireland, Scotland and the Antients had shared since 1772 and from which the Moderns had been explicitly excluded. Its renewal post Union would set a seal on the new and ongoing relationship.

Likewise **Clause 3** deals with the adherence to the 'Ancient Traditions and Principles' to entitle the fraternity to the protection of the government and the continued patronage of the House of Brunswick. After the Unlawful Societies Act of 1799 both England and Scotland would still have seen this as a priority, while Ireland was unaffected by the Act but still mindful of matters of loyalty.

---

[102] It is worth always remembering that there are many varying definitions of Pure Ancient Masonry of which the UGLE definition is only one. If one goes to South Australia their definition includes the Mark Degree as well. In 2011 they Consecrated Lodge Copernicus No.246 and the warrant has three seals and three signatures on it – those of Craft Grand Lodge, Supreme Grand Chapter and Mark Grand Lodge. It meets twelve times a year; six as a Craft lodge and three times each as a Chapter and Mark lodge. It is fascinating to see that the old styles of masonic working can still have attractions in the 21st century.

Clause 4 deals with matters of organisation. They agreed that each Grand Lodge would 'preserve its own limits' (and not trespass), it defined what military lodges could and could not do – as this was always an area where disputes got referred to Grand Secretaries. They also agreed that '…the present practice, with respect to Lodges established in distant parts under either of the THREE GRAND LODGES, shall continue on the present footing'. This would seem to refer to the Colonies where all three Grand Lodges were active but sadly it is not known what the 'present footing' actually was.

Clause 5 is a composite clause. To protect the Funds of Benevolence there would be a fee agreed among them for granting a Grand Lodge Certificate, and no automatic right of visitation, or relief, without a certificate. Certainly all three Grand Lodges would happily subscribe to this.

They also agreed, after seeing a letter 'from a person of the name of 'A. Seton.' describing himself as 'The Deputy Grand Secretary' of a Society calling themselves 'The Ulster Grand Lodge' that only members of the Grand Lodge of Ireland possessing Certificates would be admitted to any lodge. This was very much the endorsement Ireland needed to try and speed the end of the Grand East of Ulster.

Clause 6 agreed that 'it being of vital importance for the well being of the Craft' to have due regard for 'the moral character of the Individuals to be admitted' and 'their knowledge in their gradual advancement'.

On the 7th April 1814 Ireland sent a letter to London[103] setting out the attack upon freemasonry and freemasons by the Roman Catholic Church

---

[103] DGS Graham signed the letter which was written in a most clear neat secretarial hand. It complained of the persecution of freemasons by many Roman Catholic Priests in Ireland. These included the last consolations of religion refused, wives debarred purification after childbirth and infants refused baptism. The letter 'hereby authorised and required' those appointed to represent the Grand Lodge 'at the ensuing Masonic congress in London', to seek the support of those present. Thus explicitly in the 7th clause we find 'absolutely discountenancing in all their meetings every question that could have the remotest tendency to excite controversy in matters of religion, or any political discussion whatever, have no other object in view but the encouraging and fostering of every moral and virtuous sentiment'. The contents of this clause are very much in tune with the troubled social times of Catholic assaults upon freemasonry and being at war with France.

in Ireland. Thus **Clause 7** set out the nature of freemasonry, the rights of each brother 'to his own private character', and the 'absolute discountenancing in all their meetings every question that could have the remotest tendency to excite controversy in matters of religion, or any political discussion whatever'. The delegation from Ireland came charged to take up this matter, which they duly did, and it was part of the final agreement.

The final clause, **Clause 8,** was 'That these Resolutions be reported to the THREE GRAND LODGES, entered in the Records thereof, and printed and circulated to all the Lodges holding of them respectively'.

The non-compliance with the final clause is most curious. There is not a single trace of the International Compact in the minutes of either of the Grand Lodges of England or Scotland, only in Ireland was it entered in the minutes of Grand Lodge. Not a single copy has ever been found of anything circulated after the conference, so we have to assume that a general circulation of the agreed terms never happened. Clearly Ireland felt it had made real gains and thus made sure it was duly recorded, but even in Ireland there must have been some impediment to letting the terms be generally known. One might guess that the definition of 'pure Ancient Masonry' would be somewhat inflammatory among Irish brothers who were still in the throes of discord with two Grand Lodges fighting each other, a conflict that arose partly over who might control the Royal Arch. Scotland too had already decided that the Royal Arch was not part of the masonry of the Grand Lodge of Scotland and would have no wish to see the Royal Arch issue brought to the fore again.

We know that copies of the Articles of Union were sent after they were ratified on 1st December as was an invitation to be present. While one could argue that the notice was short, or that Christmas was two days prior to St John's Day, that was perhaps not the only reason for Ireland and Scotland to remain at home. Neither Scotland nor Ireland were involved in the process of the rediscovery of 'Antientness' and neither knew what was being debated and decided in London. Neither did they know quite what might happen at the events of 27th December 1813, and indeed the experiences of the Count Lagardie on the day probably demonstrated that they were right to feel concern.

A View from Scotland

While Scotland was not without its problems it had managed to turn the Unlawful Societies Act to its own benefit and exercise somewhat better control over its lodges. It had also positively put the Royal Arch and Knights Templar outside its orbit and brought Mother Kilwinning (and her daughter lodges) back into the fold of Grand Lodge. That is not to say that there had not been rebellious moments but they had been dealt with. They did wish to make clear their support for both government and monarchy, their loyalty to the United Kingdom, but in doing so would not concede their essential Scottishness.

Anyone who has visited Scottish or Irish lodges today will know that the forms and style around the central 'Landmarks' are very different and particular to each Constitution. Clearly while there is a 'Scottish Workings of Craft Masonry Complete and Accurate from Standard Authority' which is not vastly different to the English one, many lodges work very different rituals. The Scottish Ritual book perhaps says it all when at the end of the third degree it states; "In many Scottish Lodges this Alternative Working is more elaborated; but as the ceremony of the Third Degree is necessarily of considerable length, the foregoing is generally deemed sufficient. The ancient customs of the Lodge, however, should be preserved, under the direction of the R.W.M.".

It is perhaps worth considering what it was to be Scottish or Irish and part of the United Kingdom, and Murray Pittock offers a valuable insight

> One of the most important features of Scottish experience after 1707 is that the Scots were able, even when 'North Britain' dominated as a descriptor of their country at home and 'England' prevailed abroad, to be Scottish, and to organise themselves into formal and informal groupings which clearly expressed a persisting sense of self and (however mildly expressed) a dissonance from merging into imperial Britain.[104]

When the Grand Lodge of Scotland held an Extraordinary Meeting on 20th December 1813 at which as Laurie states "congratulatory resolutions were passed and ordered to be conveyed to the Grand Lodges of England on this auspicious reconciliation and re-union" there were no caveats included.

---

[104] Murray Pittock 'Dissolving the Dream of Empire: Fratriotism, Boswell, Byron and Moore' in *Journal of Irish Studies* Vol.1 No.1, p134.

A View from Ireland

It was also true, as we shall see, that Ireland needed to use this chance to make some progress with its own problems while the new United Grand Lodge of England still wished to ensure its blessing. Ireland wanted 'to co-operate in the completion of the Great Work' simply by 'effectually ascertaining and establishing a perfect Union of Obligation and Discipline to be hereafter maintained upheld and practiced throughout the Masonic World'. They wanted England to be quite clear that there were issues to be addressed before any Irish celebrations took place, as their response makes clear!

Just thirteen days after the signing of the Articles of Union in London on 13th December 1813, they had convened an Extraordinary Meeting of Grand Lodge.[105]

Grand Lodge of Ireland
On Emergency
Honble Abram Hely Hutchinson DGM on the Throne

The Grand Lodge of Ireland from the recent receipt of the Communications, and the consequent shortness of interval previous to the Festival of St John, laments that on its part Brethren cannot be appointed whose presence in London that day might with certainty be expected, but the Grand Lodge of Ireland while it regrets not being represented at the august assembly on the 27th December, is anxious to express its sincere desire to co-operate in the completion of the Great Work, so highly interesting to the Whole Fraternity and will therefore depute at any time subsequent to the 27th Inst; which their Royal Highnesses the two Grand Masters may deem most proper and convenient to appoint approved and skilful Brethren to meet those of Scotland, and the Brethren selected by the Grand Lodges of England, for the purposes of finally and effectually ascertaining and establishing a perfect Union of Obligation and Discipline to be hereafter maintained upheld and practiced throughout the Masonic World. (signed) W F Graham DGSecy.[106]

---

[105] William Lewins in his book *Her Majesties Mails* (1864) notes that the mail from London to Edinburgh took 60 hours and that the mail coaches were able "to go thither and back again in 6 days". It is interesting to reflect that second class mail today takes just as long although no horses are over-exercised to keep the mail flowing.

[106] The letter is in the archives of the Library of Freemasonry in London Ref HC 12/A/62.

While correspondence must surely have continued with Scotland there were further exchanges between England and Ireland. On 20th December 1813 William Graham DGS sent a further missive to London stating

> Brethren likely to be delegated by us, it would most suit their convenience to attend in London as shortly before the Festival of St George as would allow sufficient time for the discussion... many of the Grand Officers will then be attending their Parliamentary duties.[107]

(signed) Graham

On 3rd February there was a reply from London

> We trust we shall have the satisfaction to meet your Brothers together with Brothers from Scotland and we indulge the belief that many points of regulation for the good of the Three Sister Grand Lodges may at that time be considered and settled particularly with regard to the granting of Certificates and the recognition of the acts of one another.[108]

A careful reading of the letter of 13th December clearly reveals a determination by Ireland to seize this opportunity to get England to address other issues which were of particular concern to Ireland - not just parochial matters but things they felt to be of worldwide import. And the 20th December letter (above), just a mere week later, sets out the timescale they felt appropriate.

In Summary

The International Compact of 1814 is an unusual document in that only two known examples of the agreed text remain. The first was closeted in the Minutes of the Grand Lodge of Ireland until aired for the very first time by Bro W J Chetwode Crawley, the famous Irish Masonic historian, in 1915, effectively to celebrate the centenary of the event. The second is a draft manuscript copy in the Library and Museum of Freemasonry in London with annotations said to be in the hand of William White the Grand Secretary of the Moderns. It is kept in the library safe in its own purpose-made blue case.

Thus it becomes clear that there was a full text negotiated in advance for ratification on the 27th June; but when they met that day there were

---

[107] The letter is in the Library of Freemasonry in London HC/12/A/63.

[108] R E Parkinson, *History of the Grand Lodge of Ireland* Vol.2 (1957) p20.

changes sought by both Ireland and England. The Duke of Sussex wanted to know that his ideas about the Royal Arch were accepted and the Irish were still unhappy with the clause that dealt with religion. One might guess that the problem of producing a 'baker's dozen' of copies that day from William White's amended copy was going to be beyond the secretarial resources late in that day. Accordingly the signing was not planned to take place until the Saturday 2nd July. That presumably would allow time for clean fair copies in the best secretarial hand to be produced for signing.

No original copy signed by those present remains but the agreement reached must have served the needs of the times. Above all it was a practical mutual endorsement by the Three Home Grand Lodges of England, Ireland and Scotland of their mutual acceptability and respectability.

HRH Prince Augustus Frederick Duke of Sussex (1773-1843),
Grand Master, UGLE 1813-1843

Chapter 13 - Calm and Order appear from Confusion

Today it is possible to join a large number of masonic organisations, each with various degrees and particular messages, and importantly each one with its own Grand and Provincial organisational structures – and it is easy to think that it was always such. It was not!

It seems that freemasons have always had an appetite to experience more degrees and the early nineteenth century was no exception from this tendency. Below is a typical list of degrees worked, this one compiled by the Irish brother and ritualist John Fowler in around 1810, and found among his papers:[109]

1. Entered Apprentice, Fellow Craft, Master Mason

---

[109] W J O'Brien 'Irish Royal Arch Masonry' in *Transactions of the Chapter of Research No.222* (1978-1985) pp 85-105. The list of degrees is on p86 and followed by an explanation of them.

2. Past Master, Excellent Mason, Super Excellent Mason, Arch Mason, Royal Arch Mason

3. Ark Mason, Mark Fellow Mason, Mark Master, Link Mason or Wrestle, Babylonian Pass (or Red Cross of Daniel), Jordan Pass, Royal Order (or Prussian Blue)

4. Black Mark, Templar (Four Grades), Mediterranean Pass, Malta, Red Cross of Constantine, Knight Patmos

Fowler's list is without any comment so he was clearly familiar with all these degrees. There are other lists and while they might differ they would be equally complex. One of the problems was that only the first group of degrees had any accepted governing body. Many, often senior, members of Grand Lodges had taken these other degrees but they still remained officially disapproved of by authority. Yet a good proportion of ordinary masons in ordinary lodges were working these degrees as part of their daily masonry. Grand Lodges however saw this sort of activity as diluting the control that they were able to exercise. Only in Antients' lodges in England was the Royal Arch worked in lodges with express approval, and only in England had a Grand Chapter been created, associated with the Moderns Grand Lodge. There were Knights Templar bodies at the time, sometimes more than one, and 'distant' from any 'established authority'.

To some extent the formation of the United Grand Lodge of England (UGLE) in 1813 marked a turning point in masonic organisation. The dangers of having got things wrong had been suffered by Ireland. The confusion of multiple chartering masonic bodies and the ill feeling such as that generated during the short life of the Grand Lodge of Ulster needed to be avoided by the Grand Lodges of England and Scotland.

It seems appropriate to cover events in Ireland and Scotland, as well as England, over the next couple of decades. That background can at least in part allow a better comprehension of how matters got (partly) resolved and allow the reader to reflect and understand rather better both the considerable differences and similarities between the masonries of the nations of the British Isles.

ENGLAND

The Duke of Sussex (1773-1843) bestrode English Freemasonry for the thirty years that followed the Union, as witnessed by his masonic titles of Grand Master, United Grand Lodge of England 1813-1843; Most Excellent Z, Supreme Grand Chapter 1813-1843; and Grand Master, Grand Priory 1812-1843 (the Duke of Kent had held this office from 1805-1807). There can be no doubt that Sussex stamped his own ideas upon freemasonry as a whole and thus England does have a style that is rather different to all other constitutions. It is perhaps the anomalous position of the Royal Arch which attracts a 'bad press' for the Duke of Sussex.

It might seem strange that the matter of creating a Supreme Grand Chapter was something that was not achieved until 1817. There has been much debate and much written regarding the whys and wherefores of all this 'delay'. Alas there are no documents to guide the analysis, but perhaps it is worth reflecting that the final Craft ritual matters were not finally settled till 1816 and perhaps there was no incentive, even no permission to move on to other matters until it was completed. As Bernard Jones says, 'the crowning anomaly in the history of the Royal Arch, which is a series of anomalies, is the one implicit in the declaration of 1817 that Royal Arch masonry does not constitute a degree.' This is especially strange because for the Antients it <u>was</u> the fourth degree and for the Moderns who practised it - also a separate degree.

The whole idea of 'pure ancient masonry' also seems like a similar anomaly. Where the idea that freemasonry consists of 'only three degrees' comes from remains another mystery. Until the 1720s / 1730s there were only two degrees, and only after did they became three. Later other degrees appeared most notably the Royal Arch and Knights Templar. It was this insistence that excluded the Excellent Master degree from the Royal Arch - a great loss and which also excluded the Mark degree from having any early official status within an English freemasonry. One might argue that this has been a big loss to both masonry in England and to international portability and practice as well.

However such considerations for us today were not going to be of concern to the Duke of Sussex in 1813! His concerns were likely to be making the Union function in practice, to bring peace and especially to avoid the calamities that had befallen Ireland. The Knights Templar went into hibernation until about 1830 and the Ancient and Accepted Rite (known as the Scottish Rite in North America) was not warranted in England until 1845. True there were some memorialists (Antient masons) who disliked the changes but the only major dissent was associated with the formation of the Grand Lodge of Wigan in 1823[110].

IRELAND

The 2nd Lord Donoughmore (1757-1832) was Grand Master from 1789-1812. He came from Co. Tipperary, was a politician and a General in the British Army. He had been ready to stand down as Grand Master from 1800 but was persuaded to remain, which he did until he eventually resigned in 1812. He named as his successor the 3rd Duke of Leinster, whose father had been Grand Master in 1770, 1771 and 1777. Leinster was initiated, passed and raised on 13th June and installed Grand Master on the 23rd June 1813. At this time it was recorded that around 670 lodges were on the roll, the highest total to be achieved. In 1864 the Ulster Magazine recorded that there were 247 lodges of which 169 were in Ulster.

The Duke took over at the end of the existence of the Grand Lodge of Ulster and thus the task of bringing peace and organisation to Irish freemasonry fell upon his shoulders. He managed to gain total control of all the orders for an astounding number of years.

Grand Master, Grand Lodge of Ireland 1813-1874

First Principal, Grand Chapter 1829-1873

Grand Master, Supreme Grand Encampment 1836-1873

Head, Grand Council of Rites 1836-1873

After the attempt by Grand Lodge to take control of the Royal Arch and Knights Templar failed in 1805 it was to be some time before

---

[110] Beesley's book on the Grand Lodge of Wigan is long out of print and hard to find any copies. A new book on the subject, published in 2012 by David Harrison, *The Liverpool Masonic Rebellion and the Grand Lodge of Wigan*, should provide an up to date view of these events. The Grand Lodge of Wigan comprised six lodges and it struggled on till about 1866. One remaining lodge, the Lodge of Sincerity, continued the Grand Lodge until 1913 when it returned to the Grand Lodge of England under a new warrant No.3677.

another attempt was made. And with good reason for there were two bodies chartering Chapters: the High Knight Templars of Ireland Kilwinning Lodge, and the Early Grand Encampment of Ireland. At last in 1828 John Fowler[111] wrote to the Duke of Leinster on this matter and in June 1829 a Supreme Grand Chapter of Ireland was formed, the inaugural meeting being attended by representatives of 53 Chapters.

One matter that did not get resolved in 1829 concerned the legend of the Royal Arch, and this had to wait until 1864 for a resolution. Traditionally there had been two different legends. One involves Josiah and relates to the repair of the First Temple under King Josiah – around 855BC. The second is that of the building of the Second Temple by Prince Zerubbabel after the return of the Jews from Babylon – around 515BC. Some lodges practised one legend, some the other and indeed some offered both. In 1864 it was decided that all Royal Arch Chapters in Ireland would work the Josiah legend and so it has remained till today. Their ritual of the Zerubbabel legend then went via the Knights Templar to eventually emerge again in 1923 in the form of the Grand Council of Knight Masons.

We may, with some confidence, assume when Laurence Dermott was Exalted in 1746 that he received a legend in the which the leading character was Zerubbabel. If it had been otherwise the English history of the Royal Arch might have been infinitely more complicated.

During the 1823 suppression of meetings the Early Grand Encampment had disappeared from the scene but on 25th August 1836 a Grand Convocation of High Knight Templars was held in the rooms of the Grand Lodge of Ireland. They resolved to establish a Supreme Grand Encampment with the Duke of Leinster as Illustrious Grand Commander

---

[111] John Fowler (1769-1856) was a weaver's son and born in Dublin. He set up and ran a school in 1793 and his teaching career ran till 1836. He was initiated in 1792 and quickly proved himself an excellent ritualist. He was appointed Deputy Grand Master (DGM) in 1818 and in 1827 on the death of the previous Deputy Grand Secretary in 1827 he was appointed to that post, which he held for almost 30 years. He was an active Kilwinning Encampment member in 1806 and at this time he and John Boardman did not see eye to eye. He was active in all branches of masonry and for example had extensive correspondence with Dalcho regarding the Scottish Rite. Much of the manner of Irish ritual is believed to be due to his attention to ritual detail; this sadly was better than his business acumen.

(changed to Grand Master in 1838) and with John Fowler as Grand Registrar.

SCOTLAND

In 1810 the Royal Grand Conclave petitioned for the patronage of the Duke of Kent as Grand Master of the Templars in England. The Charter they received allowed them to 'confer the Knight Templar Grades upon those qualified as Royal Arch Masons'. Their Scottish Grand Master Alexander Deuchar saw the weakness of not having any control over the degrees preceding those of the Knights Templar. Thus in 1815 he convened a special committee involving all those in Scotland working the Royal Arch with a view to creating a Grand Body. They sought the advice of the Home Grand Lodges, especially of England after its Union of 1813. The Duke of Sussex was supportive but eventually the matter got bogged down in committee. Eventually, in August 1817, thirty four chapters met in Edinburgh and as a result a Supreme Grand Royal Arch Chapter was erected. It ended up taking various other degrees under its protection. The Mark degree, while part of Grand Chapter, is normally worked by Craft lodges under dispensation. The Supreme Grand Royal Arch Chapter of Scotland works, as part of the Holy Royal Arch, the Excellent Master degree (which was lost in England) and Mark. Also it is responsible for the Royal and Select Masters and the Lodge and Council degrees (which include both Royal Ark Mariner and Knights of the East and West degrees).

Somewhere around 1793 the Early Grand Encampment of Ireland began to issue warrants, not only in Ireland but also in England and Scotland. What perhaps moved events on was the direction from the Grand Lodge of Scotland in October 1800 'prohibiting and discharging its daughters (lodges) to hold any meetings above the degree of Master Mason, under penalty of forfeiture of their Charter'. Thus any group of masons wanting to be Knights Templar needed a warrant, and many sought them from Ireland, in particular from the Early Grand Encampment. In 1810 the Edinburgh Encampment (Warranted 1806) sought the Patronage of the Duke of Kent, who (they claim) was Grand Master of the Templars in England. This group was headed by Alexander Deuchar (1774-1844)

Matters moved on and in 1822 a pamphlet was printed in Scotland but referring to 'events' in Dublin of 11th May 1822 concerning the Early Grand Encampment. It notes the intention of 'giving every support to such warrants as have been or hereafter shall be sanctioned by this Early Grand Encampment' and that a group of Scottish Templars 'came desiring to create a Grand Encampment of High Knights Templar in Scotland and to the Early Grand Encampment of Ireland granting this prayer of the petition'. This was followed a few years later on 24th June 1826 by a Charter of Renunciation from the Irish Grand Encampment relinquishing any control over the Scottish Templars.[112]

Thus for a variety of reasons the structure of extra Craft masonry in Scotland turned out to be greatly different from that in England and much more akin to the American York Rite structure (but in Scotland excluding the Knights Templar). In England these degrees are all under different Grand Bodies representing the Mark (which includes the Royal Ark Mariners), the Royal and Select Masters, and the Allied Masonic Degrees.

Mark Masonry

There is no doubt that a degree with the name Mark attached to it was practised in England in the 18th century. However just what it comprised remains unclear. This dilemma is a common one in freemasonry and one is unwise to assume that a name alone defines the content; content of ritual can mutate within and across degrees.

The claim for the introduction of the Mark Degree as worked today seems to go to Bro John Fowler DGM (1818-24) and DGS (1827-1856 on his death). This respected brother and ritualist had received a Mark Master Mason ritual from Charleston (in South Carolina) in 1825. On 13th December 1825 Fowler at a meeting of the members of Royal Arch Lodge No.2, the oldest Chapter in Ireland, constituted a 'lawful lodge of Mark Master Masons'. Fowler appears to have revised the American ritual that he had received considerably but it gained popularity in Ireland as

---

[112] Trying to determine events in both Ireland and Scotland proves quite problematic. The explanation of the situation in Scotland relies largely upon the notes of the eminent Irish masonic researcher Philip Crossle in the documents and notes ref BR 541 CRO fol. in the Library and Museum of Freemasonry in London.

brethren came to Lodge No.2 and carried the degree back to their lodges. After this it was adopted by the Grand Royal Arch Chapter of Scotland and thence under Scottish warrants to England.[113] The story of the spread of Mark Lodges from the Bon Accord Chapter in Aberdeen to England is well recorded elsewhere[114]. From them, on 13th September 1851, a warrant was obtained for a Bon Accord Mark Lodge in London. The Mark degree was not an issue in the events around 1813 in England; its decisive moment was to come later in the nineteenth century.

Ancient and Accepted Rite

While there had been several extra Craft degrees of a 'Scottish Rite nature' being practiced by freemasons these did not take anything like their current form until the formation in 1801 of the Supreme Council in Charleston, South Carolina. They played no role in the events leading up to the 1813 Union in England, but since have become a major order in freemasonry.

There were other degrees known before the Union that continued afterwards, and some are still extant today. In general terms Ireland and Scotland had Grand Councils of Rites which acted as holding bodies for degrees that were no longer practiced or whose place was not yet clear. Today the situation is different in every jurisdiction and there always remains more to be explored by those with the interest and enthusiasm.

The process of bringing some structure to the freemasonries of the British Isles was a slow one. One might say it started in 1766 with the Royal Arch Charter of Compact but that most of the process took place in the second and third decades of the nineteenth century. However in reality the process is an ongoing and lively one – quite how many orders freemasonry can absorb has yet to be determined!

---

[113] Thomas Moorhead, 'Arches of the Years: Historical Highlights R.A.C. 2', Dublin 1825-1958 in *Transactions of the Chapter of Research No.222* (1978-1985) Vol.1 pp 48-49

[114] Peter Glyn Williams, "In the Beginning…': The Establishment of Mark Masonry in England and Wales' in *Marking Well* edited by Andrew Prescott (2006)

HRH Prince Augustus Frederick Duke of
Sussex (1773-1843),
Grand Master, UGLE 1813-1843

Francis Rawdon Hastings, Earl of Moira
(1754-1826)
Acting Grand Master Moderns 1795-1816
Acting Grand Master Scotland 1806-1808

Endwords

There cannot be a single brother in the English Constitution whose masonry is not, to this day, affected by the Union of 1813. It has left English freemasonry with a structure which is very different from the structures typically adopted elsewhere. The Duke of Sussex's legacy from the Union has not always been a particularly bright one. Pick and Knight for example say 'Although the Duke of Sussex exercised his powers in a somewhat arbitrary and dictatorial manner, who else could have retained the loyal fidelity of such (Antient) Past Deputy Grand Masters as Agar and Harper for the rest of their lives…'.

The Duke of Sussex was Grand Master for some 30 years, until his death in 1843. Ireland too had the Duke of Leinster as Grand Master from 1813-74, serving some 61 years. It is worth recalling also that these two brethren controlled every facet, every order, of freemasonry in their territories; and that there was a reason for that. The decades either side of 1800 were ones in which there was considerable thirst for and growth in the degrees beyond the three of Craft freemasonry and there was no organisation to enable those other degrees to maintain some order. These were also times of social unrest at home and war abroad. If the Hanoverians needed freemasonry to demonstrate their British credentials then perhaps freemasonry needed the monarchy to demonstrate its loyalty?

But what options were open to the Duke of Sussex and the Earl of Moira in trying to achieve Union? They knew that the Antients were in correspondence (equivalent to our recognition or being in amity) with both Scotland and Ireland and had been firmly and jointly so since 1772. They would also have known, as did the Duke of Atholl, just what the Scottish ritual and practices were – they had both been Grand Masters in Scotland.

In truth it WAS the Moderns who were out of step. They had only one option in their hunt for general acceptance in the masonic world, and that was to achieve Union. That would require reverting to something close to the Ancient Masonry practised elsewhere. It was that same imperative that made the Antients' Grand Committee insist that any deal had to be acceptable to both Scotland and Ireland. If not then the Antients would have lost everything if they became estranged from the other freemasonries of the British Isles.

The Earl of Moira was a dealmaker. Whether he had anything Masonic in mind when he was appointed to be Commander in Chief of the military in Scotland we cannot know but he arrived in September 1803 and in November of that year visited the annual meeting of the Grand Lodge of Scotland. In 1804 the Grand Lodge of Scotland took up constant correspondence with the Moderns.

> That a communication be opened between the Grand Lodge of England under the auspices of H.R.H. the Prince of Wales and the Grand Lodge of Scotland and that the necessary measures be adopted that the same friendly intercourse should take place between these Grand lodges as at present subsists between the Grand Lodge of Scotland and the Grand Lodge under his Grace the Duke of Atholl.

Scotland again had shown that it was not going to be drawn into the arguments in England between the rival Grand Lodges. There remains the thought that Moira and the Prince of Wales sought an organisational Union between the Grand Lodge of Scotland and the Moderns. The wording recorded in the minutes used by Moira, when addressing the Moderns in 1806 and when referring to Scotland, was 'his lordship had stated his firm belief that this Grand Lodge would readily concur in any measures that might be proposed for the establishment of Union and Harmony among the general body of masons'.

Consulting *The Oxford English Dictionary,* it offers two useful definitions of the word 'union'. The first is that of the act of joining or uniting one thing to another or others or two or more things together, so as to form one whole or complete body. And secondly the uniting together of the different sections, parties or individuals of a nation, people or other body so as to produce a general agreement of concord. There is also the use of the same word in a letter to the Antients from the Grand Lodge of Ireland using the phrase 'did mutually concur with a strict Union with the Antient Grand Lodge in London'. Here it is quite clear what was intended – a general agreement of concord and not a legal union of the two bodies. Likewise Moira when he says 'Union and Harmony' surely (in this context) has to mean the same. When Hamill states (on p37 of his paper) that he can find no evidence of any intention of anything other than fraternal relations I am sure he is absolutely right. Moira was using the word union in its common 19th century usage and not in the way it would normally be understood in the 21st century.

Ireland was perhaps a different matter as the United Kingdom had only been created in 1801, so the relationship was rather newer and less close. In the decade before the Union it was well known to all those involved that freemasonry in Ireland was experiencing something of a crisis. Nobody looking towards Ireland was likely to be proposing a fixed Union of Grand Lodges. It is probably fair to say that the differences in Ireland between Dublin and the Irish Counties, between North and South and between Catholic and Protestant were problems of long standing. Added to which there was of course the ambivalent relationship between those Irish who had migrated to England and settled there, and the local English population. These were the very same prejudices that had been thrown at the Antients, and the independent lodges which formed it, back in the mid eighteenth century.[115]

---

[115] These sorts of issues were not uncommon. For example in Canada the Grand Lodge of Ireland had issued a warrant for Leinster Lodge No. 283 on 1st February 1821, to meet in Kingston, Ontario, to meet the need of the Irish masons in the town. There was however already another, English, lodge in Kingston and it was not long before they were complaining that the Irish brethren's conduct 'was not orderly', that they were taking in candidates previously refused by the English lodge and doing so more cheaply.

Ireland had led the issuing of warrants to military lodges, as had the Antients in England. Many of these lodges were set up in regiments which were nominally English even though a majority of soldiers within them would have been of Irish origin. The interaction of these masons wherever they went was a cause of much aggravation and complaint to Grand Secretaries. The military lodges were also largely the means by which the various national forms of British freemasonry came to be spread around the globe

Other writers have taken views on the outcome of the Union between the Antients and Moderns. Gould in his chapter on the United Grand Lodge 1814-1885 notes 'By the Union of the two Societies a great work was accomplished, although the terms on which it was effected left many things to be desired'. In particular he notes that it was only in 1816 that agreed rituals were completed. He notes the continued support of the Past Deputy Grand Masters of the Antients, Perry, Harper and Agar for the new order. As to the leadership of the Duke of Sussex he says

> 'The Duke governed on the whole both wisely and judiciously, and though his idea of the relation in which he stood towards the Craft may best be summed up in the famous phrase *'L'etat c'est moi''.*

> 'By this time the old order of things had been succeeded by the new. The two sets of Freemasons were firmly welded together into one homogeneous whole, and the last decade of the Duke of Sussex's administration was unclouded by any revival of ancient animosities.

Why the rush to Union on 27th December 1813? Mandleberg[116] comments that 'The Duke of Sussex, never the most patient of men, was becoming tired of the prevarications, and wanted the whole matter resolved.' One has to sympathise with that viewpoint but it must be worth adding that even on the day matters of ritual and organisation were still not resolved and in some cases it was some years before they were. The Duke however did know whom he had to deal with because in his letter to Count Lagardie he describes the English brethren as 'I do not have to tell you, my dear Count, that we will need to be very prudent in

---

More on this incident can be read in J Ross Robertson *A History of Freemasonry in Canada* (1899) PDF copies of which are available online.

[116] John Mandleberg in the summary of 'Promulgation and Reconciliation' in *AQC* Vol.123 p172.

this undertaking because of the number of individuals with which I will have to deal, and the infinity of extravagant opinions amongst them'. While one might think this a convenient exaggeration by Sussex, any brother who has tried to get a group of English brethren today to agree upon any matter of ritual variation would not find such an opinion an exaggeration.[117] The speed with which the Union was finally effected feels to be one of speed and determination and that any issues remaining would be sorted out afterwards.

There remains the matter of the Royal Arch, Knights Templar and other degrees as well. Clearly the Royal Arch had to be included or it would seem highly unlikely that the Antients would have found the Union acceptable. The Templars went into hibernation as did other degrees. There would appear to have been a desire which started after the Union and step by step resolved ritual matters, dealt with the Rules and Regulations, the Royal Arch and later the Knights Templar. This would clearly have been under the control of the Duke of Sussex.

The Royal Arch in England was an organisational issue immediately after the Union, and remained a similar issue in Ireland and Scotland for a couple of decades. Even today, some two centuries later, this compromise of 1813 remains unresolved within English freemasonry. The question as to whether the Royal Arch is a degree or not, the loss of the Excellent Master degree and the Royal Arch / Mark fracture remains; all in the effort to maintain an artificial and peculiarly English definition of something called 'pure ancient masonry'.

Sussex would have taken a view on events in Ireland, especially the troubles caused by the attempt to incorporate the Royal Arch and Knights Templar and, wisely, decided not to go down a similar road and risk stirring up trouble. But some sort of compromise had to be found.

It seems to me that the Earl of Moira with his political negotiating skills and sympathy for those feeling oppressed within society was the person who managed the interactions between all the Grand Lodges to create an atmosphere where seeking a consensus leading to Union was acceptable to all parties. However he had failed to achieve Union in 1810 and his departure in the first part of 1813 to India had firmly placed the

---

117 One is reminded of the joke; '(Question) What is the difference between a terrorist and a freemason? (Answer) You can negotiate with a terrorist!'

challenge in the hands of the Duke of Sussex. Fraternal relations were achieved in 1813 and maintained with both the Grand Lodges of Ireland and Scotland – the Three Home Grand Lodges.

When I started researching this book I felt that the Duke of Sussex had not really done a good job for the Craft around 1813 and I had been almost unaware of the Earl of Moira. I now find myself full of admiration for their energy and commitment to finding a way to bring brothers of greatly differing and often strongly held opinions to a state of 'Union and Harmony' (as Moira said in 1806). It is hard to see what alternative strategies they could have employed to achieve a lasting union; and what they settled upon has endured for two centuries in the form of **The United Grand Lodge of England**.

Arms of the 1717 Grand Lodge, the Moderns

Arms of the Antients Grand Lodge

Arms of the United Grand Lodge of England pre 1919 Grant of Arms.

John Belton

Born in England and studied Microbiology at Liverpool University in the 1960s, where he was a rock climber and alpinist with first ascents to his name in the Valais Alps of Switzerland. He then returned to university and took a Masters Degree in Marketing after which he joined a multinational pharmaceutical company. This led to a career in international marketing and exporting mainly in the Middle East with excursions into advertising, logistics, and project management. He became a Freemason in 1980, Master in 1992 and is also an affiliate member of Lodge Ellangowan No.716 in Scotland and Honorary Member of the Internet Lodge of Research in Calgary, Alberta. In 1998 he was a founder of Internet Lodge No.9659 UGLE and its second master. His abiding interest in modern manifestations of the Craft is ongoing. The opportunity to be in distant places has, over the years, given him the opportunity to visit lodges in many countries. Elected as Fellow No.203 of the Philalethes Society in 2010. He is also an VIII^{0} member of the Societas Rosicruciana in Anglia.

The whole matter of the decline in masonic membership has been a theme of his research and papers on this subject have been published in *Heredom*, *AQC*, Victorian Lodge of Research (Australia) and the Southern California Lodge of Research among others and he has lectured around the world on this topic. He has been a regular contributor of articles to the English masonic magazine *The Square* over the past decade mainly dealing with issues within freemasonry. A supporter of the Centre for Research into Freemasonry, his studies with David Harrison on North West English Lodges in the Industrial Revolution has been published in their Sheffield Series in *Researching British Freemasonry 1717-2017* and he has delivered papers at both the 2007, 2009 and 2011 International Conferences on the History of Freemasonry. Current interests include the history of international recognitions among Grand Lodges and the role of fraternalism in the growth of national identity in 19th century Europe.

He lives in the Peak District in the north of England in an 18th century vernacular style stone built cottage in the hills south of Manchester and on the edges of the National Park.

Acknowledgements

It was comments by James Daniel that caused me to redirect a previous research towards the events of 1813, then talking with David Harrison who told me that I was not talking to him of a paper but of a book – so why didn't I write the book. So I did.

In the beginning I was not sure that there was a story to tell and it was the unearthing of a variety of documents that got me on the trail. The resources of the Library and Museum of Freemasonry in London have been invaluable, but perhaps more to the point no archive is of any use without helpful librarian archivists. Thus my personal thanks to Martin Cherry, Susan Snell and Diane Clements for their willingness to answer my questions and reply, on several occasions, with comments such as 'Well you might find this file worth looking through'. I do need to add thanks to Bob Cooper Librarian of the Grand Lodge of Scotland in Edinburgh and Rebecca Hayes the Librarian at the Grand Lodge of Ireland in Dublin for similar support and encouragement at various stages of the project. As a resource there is nothing to rival a set of *Ars Quatuor Coronatorum*, the Transactions of Quatuor Coronati Lodge No.2076 (EC) – mine has been well used.

Writing a history book requires not only attention to detail but also effort to try and ensure that the book is a pleasing read. To my numerous friends and encouragers who have read and commented my heartfelt thanks, but this still leaves the need for a few special mentions. To Prof Aubrey Newman of Leicester University a thank you for reading the text and providing learned comment and to Prof Andrew Prescott also, especially for his Forewords. Andrew when he was Professor at the then Centre for Research into Freemasonry at Sheffield University always managed to dig out fascinating facts and stories and to explore previously hidden masonic byways. I am sure he has provided inspiration to many others as well as myself to cast their intellectual net wider while researching.

When I hold this book in my hands I have to thank David Naughton-Shires of theimagedesigns.com for the cover. But final and special thanks have to go to Brother John Acaster. John has that very special skill of being able to edit text while also having a sound grasp of both masonic and general history. Any residual misplaced commas, co;ons (sic) etc remain the authors responsibility, a problem resulting from the laxness of too much digital communication over the decades.

Image Credits

In particular thanks are extended to the Library and Museum of Freemasonry, at The United Grand Lodge of England, Freemasons' Hall, Great Queen Street, London, and especially to librarian Martin Cherry for his help and assistance in finding suitable images. Also to Rebecca Hayes Librarian of the Grand Lodge of Ireland.

Frontispiece: The Arms of the two English Grand Lodges and underneath those of the United Grand Lodge of England prior to the Grant of Arms of 1919
> Those of the Antients and Moderns are via karenswhimsey.com and taken from *An Encyclopedia of Freemasonry and its Kindred Sciences* by Mackey and McClenacan (1912).
> Arms of United Grand Lodge, Library and Museum of Freemasonry, London

Forward: Prof Andrew Prescott

Chapter 2: Title page from *Ahiman Rezon*, Laurence Dermott (1756)
> Library and Museum of Freemasonry, London

Chapter 3: Lord Blayney
> Charter of Compact detail (1766)
> Library and Museum of Freemasonry, London

Chapter 4: 3rd Duke of Atholl
> Library and Museum of Freemasonry, London

Chapter 5: William Preston
> Library and Museum of Freemasonry, London

Chapter 6: 4th Duke of Atholl
> Library and Museum of Freemasonry, London

Chapter 7: Section of a letter from John Boardman to Thomas Harper
Library and Museum of Freemasonry, London

Chapter 8: 1st Earl Donoughmore
Library and Museum of Freemasonry, London

Chapter 9: Earl of Moira
http://en.wikipedia.org/wiki/File:Francis,_1st_Marquess_of_Hastings_%2
8Earl_of_Moira%29.jpg

Prince of Wales
Freemasons Magazine or General and Complete Library Vol II (1794)

Chapter 10: Duke of Kent
Freemasons Magazine or General and Complete Library Vol III (1794)

Chapter 11: Count de Lagardie
http://commons.wikimedia.org/wiki/File:Jacob_De_la_Gardie_%281768-
1842%29_%28from_Hildebrand,_Sveriges_historia%29.jpg

Chapter 12: John Boardman memorial plaque in St Patrick's Cathedral
Dublin
Library, Grand Lodge of Ireland, Dublin

Chapter 13: Duke of Sussex
Augustus 3rd Duke of Leinster Grand Master, Ireland
Library and Museum of Freemasonry, London

Chapter 14: Prince of Wales and Earl of Moira (see above)

Author biopic: John Belton (author) – own image

Index of Persons

CPSIA information can be obtained at www.ICGtesting.com
Printed in the USA
LVOW04s1801270115

424567LV00012B/839/P